XLA® Pocketbook

Other publications by Van Haren Publishing

Van Haren Publishing (VHP) specializes in titles on Best Practices, methods and standards within four domains:
- IT and IT Management
- Architecture (Enterprise and IT)
- Business Management and
- Project Management

Van Haren Publishing is also publishing on behalf of leading organizations and companies: ASLBiSL Foundation, BRMI, CA, Centre Henri Tudor, CATS CM, Gaming Works, IACCM, IAOP, IFDC, Innovation Value Institute, IPMA-NL, ITSqc, NAF, KNVI, PMI-NL, PON, The Open Group, The SOX Institute.

Topics are (per domain):

IT and IT Management	Enterprise Architecture	Business Management
ABC of ICT	ArchiMate®	*BABOK® Guide*
ASL®	GEA®	BiSL® and BiSL® Next
CMMI®	Novius Architectuur	BRMBOK™
COBIT®	Methode	BTF
e-CF	TOGAF®	CATS CM®
ISM		DID®
ISO/IEC 20000	**Project Management**	EFQM
ISO/IEC 27001/27002	A4-Projectmanagement	eSCM
ISPL	DSDM/Atern	IACCM
IT4IT®	ICB / NCB	ISA-95
IT-CMF™	ISO 21500	ISO 9000/9001
IT Service CMM	MINCE®	OPBOK
ITIL®	M_o_R®	SixSigma
MOF	MSP®	SOX
MSF	P3O®	SqEME®
SABSA	*PMBOK® Guide*	
SAF	Praxis®	
SIAM™	PRINCE2®	
TRIM		
VeriSM™		
XLA®		

For the latest information on VHP publications, visit our website: www.vanharen.net.

XLA® Pocketbook

Marco Gianotten

Van Haren
PUBLISHING

XLA Consortium

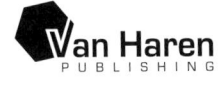

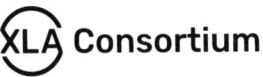

Colophon

Title: XLA® Pocketbook
Author: Marco Gianotten
Content editor: Mark Smalley
Publisher: Van Haren Publishing, 's-Hertogenbosch, www.vanharen.net
Graphic design: Overhaus, Amsterdam
DTP: Coco Bookmedia, Amersfoort
ISBN Hard copy: 978 94 018 1000 5
ISBN eBook (pdf): 978 94 018 1001 2
ISBN ePub: 978 94 018 1002 9

Edition: First edition, first impression, April 2023
Copyright: Van Haren Publishing

The XLA Consortium is an open platform that enables front-runner organizations in the emerging field of experience management (XM). Together, we fuel innovation and set standards for the digital Experience Economy.

Although this publication has been composed with most care, neither author nor publisher can accept any liability for damage caused by possible errors and/or incompleteness in this publication.
No part of this publication may be reproduced in any form by print, photo print, microfilm or other means without written permission by the publisher.

Contents

About this book 7

1 Introduction 11
2 Business Case for Better IT Service Experience 19
3 IT Service Experience and its Management 31
4 Organization of IT Service Experience Management 55
5 Transformation of the IT Service Management Organization 75

Glossary 91
Acknowledgements 123

About this book

The XLA Pocketbook introduces the concept of "Xperience Level Agreement" (XLA) and the XLA 6P Framework for understanding and applying IT service experience management. The pocketbook is intended for IT service providers and consumers who want to learn the basics of XLA in order to derive more value from IT services. Value from IT services is usually expressed in terms of efficiency or effectiveness. Organizations are more efficient when information processing has been automated. They are more effective when IT services provide new information that enables them to take – and act upon – better decisions. Traditional IT Service Management often focuses too much on technology and not enough on its impact upon people and their business. The underlying assertion is that investment in IT service experience and its business impact fosters more meaningful, rewarding, and productive work.

IT service is where value is actually realized. The moment of truth is when people experience the IT solution and benefit from it. Even if IT solution design, application development, and IT operations were executed perfectly, an inadequate IT solution generates limited value. There is also value leakage when IT solution design and application development spend more time than necessary enabling the right IT service experience. Experience Management (XM) is therefore an integral part of IT solution design and application development, as well as IT Service Management. Although most of this pocketbook is written in the context of IT Service Management, IT solution designers and application developers will understand that their contribution to the right IT service experience is crucial. They can apply empathy and focus on ensuring that there is "experience inside" their valuable contributions.

The XLA Pocketbook is based on the XLA 6P Framework. The vendor-neutral XLA Consortium is tasked with developing the XLA 6P Framework and promoting its effective adoption. This knowledge-sharing organization elicits feedback from the organizations that use the XLA 6P Framework and uses their feedback for future versions of the framework.

The XLA Pocketbook includes:
– Examples of the application of XLA
– An introduction to the XLA 6P Framework
– An overview of the key XLA concepts
– The XLA template
– The official Giarte XLA glossary of terms

It is structured in chapters that address:
1. Introduction to XLA and the XLA 6P Framework
2. Business Case for Better IT Service Experience (why)
3. IT Service Experience and its Management (what)
4. Organization of IT Service Experience Management (who)
5. Transformation of the IT Service Management Organization (how)

Chapter 1 gives a history of XLA and introduces the XLA 6P Framework that provides a way of thinking (perspectives), a way of working (practices and products), and a way of being (people, principles and propositions).

Chapter 2 is about the importance of co-creating value with customers through IT service management. It proposes the Xperience Level

Agreement as an effective instrument through which to improve customer value.

Chapter 3 is about the increasingly higher demands people place on providing and consuming IT services and explains how a better IT service experience has a positive business impact.

Chapter 4 describes the organizational structure and other resources needed to adopt and practice IT service experience management as an integrated part of IT Service Management.

Chapter 5 describes an approach for adopting IT service experience management and embedding it into IT service management activities.

1
Introduction

From software rebels creating the Agile Manifesto in a ski resort in Utah in 2001 to Steve Jobs launching the first iPhone in 2007 – the experience economy has influenced the last twenty years of Enterprise IT. However, experience had not been included in the contracting of IT services until Giarte created the Xperience Level Agreement (XLA) in 2015. In 2022, Giarte introduced the XLA 6P Framework for IT providers and consumers who want to derive greater value from IT services. This chapter gives a short overview of the history of XLA and summarizes the XLA 6P Framework.

1.1 History of XLA

ITIL was developed at the end of the 1980s to streamline and optimize service processes. In the following decade, design thinking was showcased by IDEO for creative problem-solving. The origins of Scrum for cross-team collaboration on projects also go back to the 1990s. In 1999, Joseph Pine and James Gilmore brought us the "return on experience" with their bestseller *Welcome to the Experience Economy*. Two years later, a group of software rebels gathered in a ski resort, defining the Agile Manifesto as a declaration of independence for software coding. Donald Norman published his book *Emotional Design* in 2003, after his earlier masterpiece *The Design of Everyday on User-centered Design*. In 2007, Steve Jobs performed the best product launch ever with the iPhone, setting the tone for the consumerization of Enterprise IT. Enterprise IT refers to the IT services that support large organizations. The above may seem like a random listing of events, but when connecting the dots, these developments set in motion the movement of XLA.

The notion of XLA was introduced in 2007 by Dutchman Marcel Broumels. This term, then described as Experience Level Agreement (ELA), was coined in his study on a new approach for facility management. The outcome of his study about the value of Service Level Agreements (SLA) in facility management proved relevant for the IT Service Management domain.

Unmistakably, this concept of XLA was based on Pine and Gilmore's book *The Experience Economy* (1999). The authors proposed a new way of connecting with customers and securing their loyalty. They describe the progression of economic value through agrarian, industrial, and service and experience economies. Although the concept of the experience economy was initially focused on business, it has crossed into other fields such as tourism, architecture, nursing, and urban planning.

All these and many other great moments, brilliant philosophies, and groundbreaking publications triggered the conception of the XLA movement. Putting Customer Experience and business impact at the heart of IT by collaboration was Giarte's mission. Giarte coined the term Xperience Level Agreement. Inspired by the Occupy movement, it started with activist slogans: "Users are no losers!", "We are the 99 percent!", "SLA stands for secrets, lies, and assumptions!". This provocative start transitioned into a period of scribbling models and writing articles on how to use XLA as a force for good. In 2015, Marco Gianotten, the founder of Giarte, took XLA to the Pink Elephant conference in Las Vegas, the most prominent IT Service Management conference in the world. What happens in Vegas never stays in Vegas, and a coalition of the willing started flocking together with Giarte as a safe haven. Today, this role is fulfilled by the XLA Consortium. In 2016, Gianotten published the book *Digital Empathy: When Tech Meets Touch*. After this publication, many organizations wanted to try XLA and its good practices – often as a last resort to solve problems.

In 2018, the Royal Netherlands Standardization Institute (NEN), Giarte and three external stakeholders started developing a Netherlands Technical Agreement (NTA) defining the basic requirements for XLA. The NTA 8038 document was published in 2020. The next step for a federated international standard is a Dutch NEN Standard with broader stakeholder representation to publish an authoritative standard. This NEN 8038 Standard will be published in 2023, five years after the initial NTA. This will be a steppingstone for the worldwide federation of national standardization bodies in the International Organization for Standardization (ISO). The major difference between an XLA Standard and the XLA 6P Framework, as described in this book, is that the standard focuses on the requirements for organizations that adopt XLA. The XLA 6P Framework offers guidance on how to fulfill these requirements. As such, they are closely related.

People in IT talk about adoption, usability, and productivity. They preach transformation, innovation, and software eating the world. So what? How does this affect people outside IT who use technology? What does this all mean to normal human beings? The XLA Consortium is on a sensemaking mission by simplifying IT and giving meaning to change. It is not easy. There are ill-defined "wicked" problems to be tackled, with no right or wrong solution. This requires unconventional approaches. The XLA Consortium is building the plane while flying on the XLA 6P Framework. One of the most complex parts is to codify dynamic and evolving practices.

1.2 The XLA 6P Framework

The XLA 6P Framework provides guidance to help organizations improve the impact of IT services on people and their business. It comprises a way of thinking (perspectives), a way of working (practices and products), and a way of being (people, principles and propositions).

The way of working is referred to as Experience Management (XM). This is based on the concept of consensus between IT service providers and consumers regarding the desired human experience and business impact: Xperience Level Agreement (XLA).

The XLA 6P Framework is for IT service providers and consumers who want to derive more value from IT services. It is for managers and practitioners concerned with the strategic value of IT services, with the engagement and agreement between providers and consumers, or with the operational service interactions. It is equally relevant for business functions that acquire and consume IT services, for an organization's IT department or function, and for managed IT service providers or other external IT service providers.

The XLA 6P Framework was initially developed by Giarte in the Netherlands in 2022. The vendor-neutral XLA Consortium has endorsed and adopted the XLA 6P Framework. This knowledge-sharing organization is tasked with the further development of the framework and the promotion of its effective adoption. The framework is intended to help people improve the quality of experience during the provision and consumption of IT services. It is positioned in the context of IT Service Management and applies to adjacent domains such as Agile software development and digital product management. Key driving beliefs behind the framework are people over technology, perception over facts, and direction over destination.

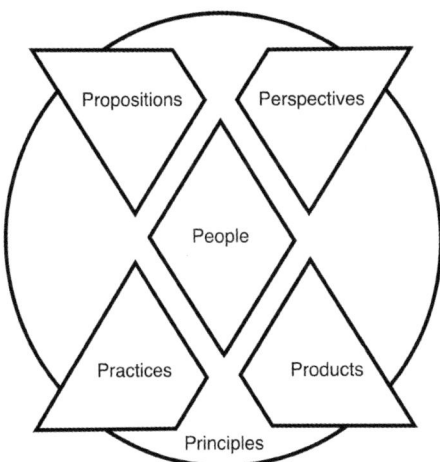

FIGURE 1

The XLA 6P Framework

The XLA 6P Framework comprises:

- **Principles:** assumptions that enable and constrain behavior in the XLA domain.

  For example, the impact of IT on people and their business defines the value of IT.

- **Propositions:** reasons for adopting XLA.

  For example, better IT services contribute to meaningful and rewarding work, which benefits people and profit.

- **Perspectives:** ways of thinking for value-creation with XLA.

  For example, experience is related to specific service interactions (in time), and to the cumulative memory of experiences of multiple service interactions (over-time).

- **People:** the organizational function that works with XLA.

  For example, the skill of empathy: the ability to relate to the feelings of others, but also to understand their thoughts, experiences, and challenges.

- **Practices:** guidance on how to adopt and execute XLA.

  For example, The Chef's Table (described in Sub-section 4.2.10) which ensures that the right stakeholders are involved, or Key Proudness Indicators that help to design value metrics which motivate people without fear and punishment.

- **Products:** digital resources that support the way of working with XLA.

  For example, a Digital Experience Monitoring (DEM) platform to proactively manage end-user experience. Subjective Experience Indicators (XIs), such as reliability, recoverability, and usability, enhance the value of DEM.

The practices are applied within the XLA Practice Areas, see Figure 2.

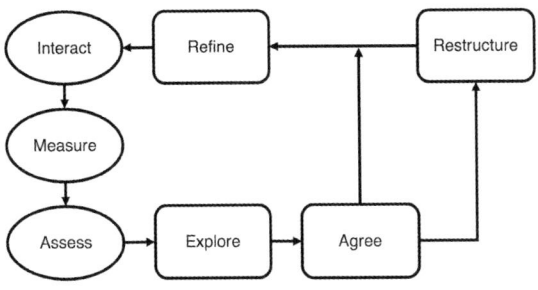

FIGURE 2

The XLA Practice Areas

- **Interact** between consumer and provider:
  For example, applying cognitive empathy by a service agent to establish where a customer is in their customer journey, and anticipating the customer's information requirements by providing the information with next steps before the customer asks for it.
- **Measure sentiment**, performance and context:
  For example, using a survey to capture users' judgments and feelings regarding the ease of use of a website.
- **Assess data** for problem areas:
  For example, comparing the survey results with the agreed goal "consistently quick and easy service" and deciding that action is needed.
- **Explore** the problem and possible solutions:
  For example, exploring the problem behind a sub-standard IT service and defining possible solutions such as tighter SLA KPIs, and more empathetic interactions.

- **Agree** on the best solution:
  For example, deciding that, after looking at the pros and cons of the possible solutions, the SLA should be extended to include the XLA goal of striving for "consistently quick and easy service."
- **Restructure** the operating model:
  For example, introducing a new role in a product team to understand user behavior regarding the product better.
- **Refine** the way of working within the operating model:
  For example, adjusting a "customer effort score" indicator to measure the improvement in scores rather than absolute individual scores.

The XLA Practice Areas are areas of work for managing the impact of IT services on people and their business. The areas support the IT service management domain as described in ITIL®, IT4IT™ etc. They also support adjacent domains such as Agile software development, and digital product management.

The XLA 6P Framework is referenced throughout the book with the intention of helping the reader understand how the various parts are related to each other.

2
Business Case for Better IT Service Experience

Why should people care about experience? This chapter is about the importance of aiming at co-creating value with customers through IT Service Management. It proposes Xperience Level Agreement (XLA) as an effective instrument to improve customer value.

The chapter covers:
- The experience economy and its relationship with enterprise IT.
- The need to understand how customer value commodities differ from non-commodity services.
- The paradoxical response that is needed to break out of traditional IT Service Management thinking.
- The application of XM in the context of IT Service Management.
- The use of Xperience Level Agreements to extend the scope of Service Level Agreements to address collaboration, experience, and business impact of services.

- Value as the common factor between ITIL, Agile, and XLA.
- Reasons to invest in XLA.

2.1. Customer Experience

When delivering a service in IT Service Management, it is essential to understand what customers experience: what is of value to the customer? What services can a service provider offer to the customer? And how can they efficiently work together to get the best value from these services? Since its emergence in the 1980s as a distinct IT domain rather than an undefined part of IT operations, IT Service Management has significantly evolved. Traditionally in ITIL, the agreements between provider and customer were documented in a Service Level Agreement (SLA). In the past, the emphasis in SLAs was on metrics that could be easily measured, such as velocity, backup recovery, downtime, and transaction speed. Reports on service delivery focused on the number of calls, requests handled in time or not, throughput time, and system availability, among other topics.

In practice, however, customers are increasingly dissatisfied with IT services, despite all the formal agreements in the SLA being met. In other words: the customer does not experience adequate value. The concept of the traditional SLA does not meet the requirements of new generations of customers regarding value. Essential new aspects of customer value are co-creation, partnering, user satisfaction, usability, and client satisfaction.

The co-creational nature of service has implications for both service consumer and provider. They are also active participants and determine, together with the service provider, how much value is derived from the service. Whereas the service provider is responsible for service output, the customer is responsible for service outcomes. Both parties are responsible for constructive collaboration.

> ### Watermelon Effect
> This metaphor illustrates where service providers show "green" performance indicators, but the customer's emotions are colored "red." The watermelon effect kicks in because traditional performance indicators such as availability, network latency, and resolution times are abracadabra for business stakeholders and end-users. A key mission of XLA is to transform watermelons into grapes: green on the inside and outside, and nice and small. This insight led to the recognition of the human being behind the various organizational roles such as client, user, manager and professional. Simply put, the adagio is: "In IT Service Management the focus is on improving the way people work together."

2.2 Experience Economy and Enterprise IT

The experience economy is not only about experience as a distinct value proposition that people are prepared to pay for, but also about the impact that experience with products and services has on work and personal life. These are key messages in the book *The Experience Economy* by Pine and Gilmore, as mentioned in the introductory chapter of this book.

Characteristic examples of user and Customer Experience in IT are:
- The accessibility and user-friendliness of the IT support.
- The IT service is easy to understand and easy to use.
- The onboarding goes effortlessly.
- The flexibility in the cooperation between IT and their customers.
- The proactive approach of the IT provider in offering new solutions that support the customer's business.

Why are user and Customer Experience also the next thing in Enterprise IT? IT is no longer just a corporate function for the digital transformation of businesses. Human beings should no longer be seen as submissive users but as self-confident digital creatives. IT professionals should ask questions such as: do ordinary people in the workplace have fun with IT? Do their experiences with IT contribute to their happiness? Have they reached the next level of digital savviness? Do they feel productive? If the answers are no, the business case for "experience first" is compelling: people transform organizations, with technology facilitating their success or failure.

2.3 What do Customers Want?

Many of today's encounters with digital technology at work or at home are framed by expectations of must-do or must-have qualities. Flaky internet, non-responsive applications, crashed computers, and rude service desk agents will drive end users crazy. Failure to provide these basic expectations causes instant dissatisfaction. But there is no upside: users aren't particularly impressed when things work as they should. It's just how things should be.

So, when is there an upside, an opportunity to impress the user? The user can be impressed when the service has not yet become a commodity, such as Wi-Fi slicing. This technology makes home networks application-aware and ensures that people can work online continuously while moving from room to room. This is an opportunity to pleasantly surprise the user until they get used to it and the feature becomes a commodity.

To satisfy customers, the provider not only needs to understand their problems before understanding the solutions they require, such as better performance, higher reliability, more convenience, improved usability, and easier accessibility. They also need to understand when there is an upside – a chance to impress the customer with a seamless experience.

2.4 Paradoxical Response

With so many disgruntled customers of IT services, IT Service Management needed a paradoxical response. When people distrust their contract partner, the classical behavior in traditional SLAs is to add more control mechanisms: introduce more rules, metrics, and heavier punishments. These control mechanisms ultimately negatively impact the collaboration and relationship between the customer and IT provider, the customer's business impact, and the end user's experience. Traditional SLAs have almost no positive impact on the quality experienced by the user or the performance of business operations.

Understanding the problem is the first step to creating a suitable solution. That is why Giarte started laying the foundation for the XLA movement with seemingly absurd or self-contradictory interventions, such as awards for toxic KPIs, Complete Waste of Time assessments, and the use of a ritual Hate List (to be burned or shredded to clear the air). Giarte coined "Secrets, Lies and Assumptions" as an alternative explanation of the abbreviation SLA. The true paradox here is that IT is meant to be used by people – but the starting point is technology. That should be the other way around: people come first.

2.5 Experience Management

In IT Service Management, the concept of Experience Management (XM) is relatively new and gaining attention quickly. XM aims to identify and understand the required Customer Experience and make adequate agreements in the form of an XLA. It also aims to transform IT delivery in that direction by continuously measuring and improving experience. XM not only implies a change in the processes and tools, but also in the attitude and skills of the professionals involved and how IT Service Management is organized.

The ultimate aim, expressed through the term "customer value", is no longer about creating an output but rather about creating an outcome. In other words: create a positive impact on people and their business. The term "experience" in XLA stresses the importance of agreements based on Customer Experience and the contribution to the outcomes that represent customer value.

Experience Management is not exclusive to the IT discipline. There are other disciplines that have practiced XM far longer than IT, such as hospitality and healthcare. When an IT function in such organizations adopts XM, the IT function's practices should be aligned with practices in non-IT functions.

Most of the guidance regarding improved Customer Experience also applies to the service provider. Their experience is equally important

– not only for themselves as individuals and employees but also for its impact on their collaboration with the service consumer.

Dutch Bank Case

Rewind to Easter 2016. Banks in the Netherlands and the interbank payment system closed from Friday, March 25th until Tuesday, March 29th, or four consecutive days. The Thursday before Easter, a Dutch bank processed scheduled pay runs for its corporate clients. Due to a batch clean-up failure, over 110,000 salary payments were stalled over the holiday weekend. This unfortunate coincidence resulted in unhappy customers and caused severe issues for many people's monthly direct debits, such as mortgage or rent payments and healthcare insurance. The bank worked with a 99.95 percent availability KPI but did not have any business impact metrics. In the aftermath of this major incident, a meaningful dialogue emerged between the bank and its clients about risk appetite and the most critical moments of performance. Business counterparts were not expecting 100 percent uptime and availability - they knew that eliminating risks comes at a cost. They wanted to focus on business impact and Customer Experience, not on more meaningless technical metrics. The new KPI, "Perfect Pay Run", was one of the outcomes of this dialogue. The result was a reduction in the number of major incidents from 44 to 14 in the following year.

2.6 XLA and SLA

The terms "SLA" and "XLA" refer to documents in which expectations and agreements between an IT service provider and a customer are formalized. An SLA describes the IT services required and the expected level of these services. An XLA extends the scope of the output-oriented SLA to describe the collaboration, experience, and business impact associated with these IT services – the outcome. See Section 3.6.4 for the definition of XLA and its explanation.

Documents do not make mistakes. But often they are the reason for conflicts between parties involved. One of the main reasons is that these documents are not updated when circumstances change. Since User and Customer Experience are becoming increasingly important, there must be frequent and meaningful communication about the User and Customer Experience, and pre-emptive and corrective measures. These documents are no longer static but have become dynamic entities.

2.7 Value in XLA, Agile and ITIL

The focus on customer value is not just an IT Service Management issue. Most IT disciplines regard value as the new normal. Take the first principle in the Agile Manifesto: "Our highest priority is to satisfy the customer through early and continuous delivery of valuable software." In ITIL® 4, the first guiding principle is: "Focus on value: everything the organization does should link back, directly or indirectly, to value for itself, its customers, and other stakeholders."

So, while the direction is clear – it's about value – few people can define the term value as something crisp and countable. Value is about perceived benefits, but the term is still vague and too abstract to understand its emotional impact. XLA makes value more tangible by looking at two related aspects: valuable and valued. Valuable is about perceived benefit to stakeholders such as customers, employees, and business managers. Valued is about being appreciated by the stakeholders and therefore feeling useful. The common denominator is that the human experience defines value. Uniquely and phenomenologically, each person experiences a service differently and, for each person, each of their experiences differs.

2.8 Reasons to Invest in XLA

Although most people adopt XLA because it just feels right, they usually justify their decisions because it helps them:
- Simplify business-IT alignment with outcome-based performance.
- Improve human-centricity in the design and delivery of all IT services.
- Maximize the usability of business application investments.
- Welcome new employees with the perfect IT onboarding.
- Foster a productive and happy workforce with hybrid workstyles.

These are universal reasons for an organization or department to invest in XLA. Depending on the type of organization they work for, they may emphasize generic benefits and some additional specific benefits.

System Integrator:
- Maximize usability in business application management.
- Bring extreme focus on business value in application transformation.
- Guarantee the best experience with cloud-native applications.

Managed Service Provider with single point of contact responsibility:
- Deliver "no hassle" for end-users in first, second and third-line support.
- Support workplace productivity by supporting workstyles.
- Monetize the business impact of mission-critical IT.

IT department:
- Welcome new employees with the perfect IT onboarding.
- Foster a productive and happy workforce with hybrid workstyles.
- Simplify business-IT alignment with outcome-based performance.

Product-centric IT (self-organization):
- Understand and act on the real impact of tech on the core business.
- Embed "experience engineering" in all product teams.
- Align key value indicators per team towards Customer Experience.

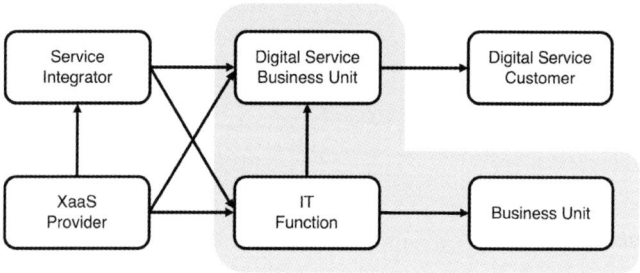

FIGURE 3

Types of organizations that benefit from XLA

2.9 Key XLA Concepts

This section defines and describes the key concepts for the reasons to invest in XLA. Other concepts such as experience, XM, and XLA that are mentioned in this chapter are described in more detail in the following chapter. This concept is listed below within the relevant element of the XLA 6P Framework.

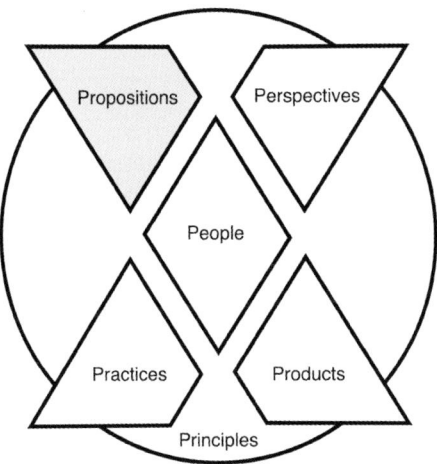

FIGURE 4

Relevant elements of the XLA 6P Framework

- Propositions:
  - Generic reasons to adopt XLA, independent of the organizational context.
  - Specific reasons to adopt XLA, depending on the organizational context.

2.9.1 Propositions

Propositions are the reasons that people use to justify their investments in XLA. See Section 1.2 for an example.

3
IT Service Experience and its Management

What is XLA and Experience Management? The previous chapter explained the importance of shifting the focus from technology to consumer experience. This chapter is about the increasingly higher demands people place on how they feel about providing and consuming IT services and how a better IT service experience has a positive business impact.

The chapter covers:
- The difference in expectations from Enterprise IT services compared with consumer technology.
- The fact that service experience is equally important for service agents as for their customers.
- The strategic value of highly engaged professionals in an outsourcing relationship.
- The belief that Enterprise IT should aim for a quality of experience that is good enough rather than delightful.
- Definitions and descriptions of key XLA concepts that are covered in this chapter.

IT can allow for an excellent experience. Whether people use a product (such as a notebook or a business application), or participate in a process (e.g., the handling of a service ticket or onboarding), experience can greatly impact their perception of services. There is also a logical, economic reason to manage experience. Why spend millions of euros on application development when users hate the new and shiny? The real Return on Investment (ROI) is successful adoption by the customer. Customers and clients all have strong feelings when it comes to IT. When mission-critical IT systems fail, "outage" and "outrage" are interchangeable. That is why the terms Experience Management (XM) and Return on Experience Investment (ROXI) were introduced in XLA.

3.1 Enterprise IT is no Disney World

In the entertainment industry, people pay for a memorable experience. Customer Experience is a distinctive economic value driver. Enterprise IT is no Disney World: experiences cannot be seen independently of products and services. At Disney World, it doesn't really matter which attractions a customer experiences – they will always have a fun day. With Enterprise IT, however, the product or service is crucial: MS Excel cannot be replaced by MS PowerPoint, no matter how enjoyable the experience is.

After Apple introduced the iPhone and other companies introduced similar smartphones, many employees preferred these mobile devices over the IT departments' corporate-issued phones. The superior User Experience of consumer technology influenced employees' attitudes and expectations towards the modern-day concept of Enterprise IT.

As such, consumers of Enterprise IT services are increasingly sensitive to how they are treated. The design of services and customer journeys influence user satisfaction and purchasing behavior. Consumer Experience is getting more critical. The underlying IT services, however, are still the primary economic value driver. Yet, experiences can be a dominant differentiator. The perfect launch of new IT services, the successful landing of a digital transformation project in the business, the ease of getting service requests fulfilled, and the peace of mind that problems will not occur again – these are all experiences that add significant value.

3.2 Experience is a Two-way Street

When the Covid-19 pandemic hit in 2020, the grand shift to remote working happened almost overnight. Employees had to connect remotely to their applications and data using a VPN and swiftly needed to adopt collaboration tools. The IT service desk was on the front line of these rapid developments. Service desk agents also had to adjust to their new remote working environment. Suddenly they found themselves without onsite support or co-workers to help them out. Organizations did everything to carry on "as usual", but the impact of the sudden move to remote working was massive for service desks: there were more tickets, which in turn increased resolution times, ticket backlogs, and stress among service desk agents.

Hence, experience is not just something that relates to the customer. Employee Experience (EX) is equally important. Customer Experience (CX) reflects Employee Experience (EX). EX is often a leading indicator for CX. If an IT organization or business unit does not manage their affairs well for their employees, they won't get it right for their IT service customers. Happy employees are more likely to spark positive customer experiences.

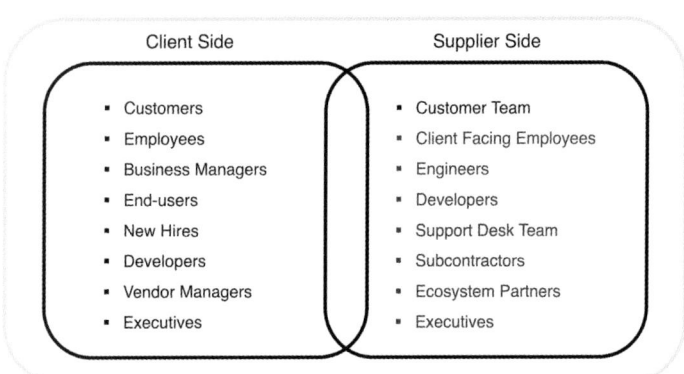

FIGURE 5

Human experiences in outsourcing relationships

3.3 With Outsourcing, EX + EX = CX

Fast forward to IT outsourcing: the client's CX depends on the supplier's EX. Experiences are a two-way street at multiple levels in the relationship between a client and their supplier of IT services, see Figure 6. With hybrid working as the new normal and the needs of employees to be productive and engaged in the digital age, people have to rethink how to address and improve the Employee Experience of those who consume IT solutions and services, and those who design and deliver them. With the outsourcing of the digital workspace, two types of employee experience must be addressed: the customer-facing employees of the service provider and the employees of the customer. They depend on the solutions and services provided. In short, it's EX + EX. IT solutions and services influence the EX of the employees (end-users). The EX of the end-users impacts the Customer Experience in the outsourcing relationship. For service providers, it's a triple win when they improve their employees' EX, the EX of their customers' employees, and the CX of the managers on the client side. In conclusion, the winning "formula" is EX + EX = CX.

For example, when the client's employees are satisfied with the IT service desk and the people helping them with service requests and fixing problems, end-user satisfaction and service agent experience correspond. When IT developers are satisfied with the landing zone provided by the engineers of the external cloud service provider, developer happiness and engineer experience communicate. When, in handling constructive conflicts, parties trust each other and share their stressors and how they best feel supported, the experience of both parties' executives corresponds.

More than ever, the engagement of the employees of an IT organization or business unit is a strategic objective. This is because engaged professionals lead to long-term employee retention, higher performance, improved quality of work, and successful partnerships. EX and CX are different sides of the same coin.

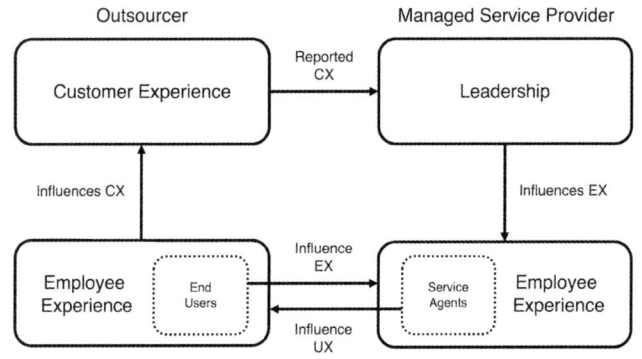

FIGURE 6

Human experiences in outsourcing relationships: EX + EX = CX

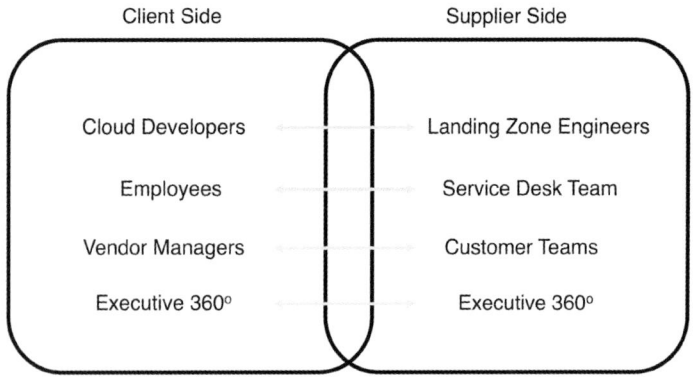

FIGURE 7

Human experience alignment between business (client side) and IT (supplier side)

3.4 Delight is Not the Goal

When an IT organization or business unit delivers a new application release or another user-impacting change "On Time and On Budget", this does not automatically mean that end-users will be satisfied and work more productively with the change. The Dutch Railways embraced the slogan "On Time, On Budget, and On Experience". The use of the term experience demonstrates that for the Dutch Railways, it is evident that Customer Experience is equally important as the "classic" goals of being on time and on budget.

To determine if experience needs to be dominant in the design, it is critical to assess consumers' expectations. "Essential quality" and "attractive quality" are two distinctive types of quality. People expect things to work. Flaky internet, underpowered notebooks, and shaky applications will drive consumers towards the brink of madness.

The purpose of Enterprise IT is not to design services for the customer's delight. Instead, the aim is to prevent terrible experiences. By determining the "Zone of Good Enough", the experience bandwidth reaches from adequate to desired as the accepted standard. People place increasingly higher demands on how they feel about providing and consuming services, so there is a business benefit in managing experience better. There is a link between decent Customer Experience and the business impact of IT.

3.5 Zone of Good Enough

In our experience economy, people often assume that customer loyalty will improve by exceeding expectations. To delight a customer is all about triggering a highly positive emotional reaction. When an organization is not Disney World nor the Carlton-Ritz, it's probably not the best move to aim for delighting their customers. It's challenging and expensive for an organization when Customer Experience is not their distinct economic offering. When an organization goes for a "wow", they must keep investing in exceeding ever-higher expectations.

A very negative experience is more persistent than an extremely positive one. That is why it is often better to prevent "downers." Welcome to the Zone of Good Enough. Instead of delight, it is better to avoid disappointment consistently. The best way is to design effortless experiences, especially when customers face problems.

A poor experience is one of the biggest reasons why customers churn, or employees check out. Most customers leave companies due to bad customer service experience. There are six experience subzones: angry, frustrated, tolerated, acceptable, satisfied, and delighted. When an experience is tolerated, acceptable or satisfied, it is in the Zone of Good Enough. When customers or employees get frustrated, the organization has missed the Zone of Good Enough.

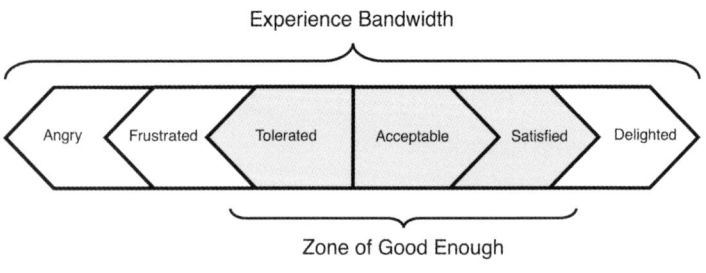

FIGURE 8

Zone of Good Enough

How to determine the Zone of Good Enough?
- Collect user stories about negative and frustrating experiences. Find patterns and similarities to identify the Zone of NOT Good Enough.
- Ask how these bad experiences happened and what can be done to prevent them in the future. Test what the outcome will be in the Zone of Good Enough.
- Connect the stories to the three subzones within Zone of Good Enough. What can be done to move one subzone in the right direction?

3.6 Key XLA Concepts

This section defines and describes the key concepts and their definitions for experience and XM. It also explains how these XLA concepts are related to each other. These concepts are listed below within the relevant elements of the XLA 6P Framework.

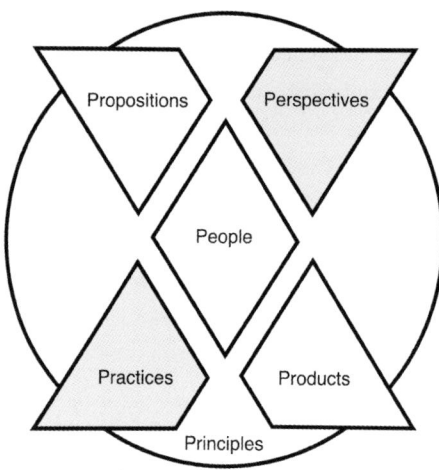

FIGURE 9

Relevant elements of the XLA 6P Framework

- **Perspectives:**
  - **Service:** economic exchange where actors in the role of service providers and service consumers collaborate to co-create value for mutual benefit.
  - **Experience:** the set of emotions, feelings, and judgments that result from sensory perception while living through an event.
  - **Xperience Level Agreement:** an outcome-oriented document; a measurable and verifiable agreement between the IT provider and the customer with respect to collaboration, experience, and business impact (the three XLA value drivers).
  - **XLA metrics:** the XLA goals, Experience Indicators, and X-data that measure and assess IT service experience.

- **Practice Areas:**
  - **Experience Management:** the set of activities that achieves better experience and greater business impact by driving and improving collaboration. It manifests itself across all XLA Practice Areas within the context of the current organization of Experience Management (modifying the current organization of Experience Management is part of the Experience Management Journey).

3.6.1 Service

Although most people would position the service economy on a timeline after the manufacturing economy, service predates manufacturing. Before labor-saving devices, or goods, were made, people needed other people to do things for them. This is the essence of service: the application of skills and resources for mutual benefit. In current service terms, this is referred to as a performance. Service also occurs in the form of an affordance – where the provider gives the consumer the right to use the provider's resources.

During the manufacturing era (c. 1850 -1980), service was needed to enable the purchase and use of goods. Providers often underestimated its value and considered it a necessary evil that distracted them from their core activities. Customers also expected that it was included in the price. The emergence of goods not only enabled customers to replace their servants – it also gave service providers more resources with which to provide new services, resulting in the current service economy that now represents at least 70 percent of most developed nations' GDP. In the second half of the twentieth century, driven by many forces including the Nordic School of Service Marketing, service was recognized as an economic and marketing research area distinct from goods. This resulted in insights into the co-creational nature of service, and the dimensions of service quality. This continued into the early twenty-first century, with the formulation of service-dominant logic and service science, as developed by Vargo and Lusch, Spohrer and others.

Current thinking in IT Service Management reflects these developments, with ITIL® 4 defining service as "a means of enabling value co-creation by facilitating outcomes that customers want to achieve, without the customer having to manage specific costs and risks." The XLA 6P Framework is also consistent with current insights, defining service as "economic exchange where actors in the role of service providers and service consumers collaborate to co-create value for mutual benefit." The XLA 6P Framework focuses on experience associated with digital and IT services.

The XLA 6P Framework applies to experience associated with digital and IT services.

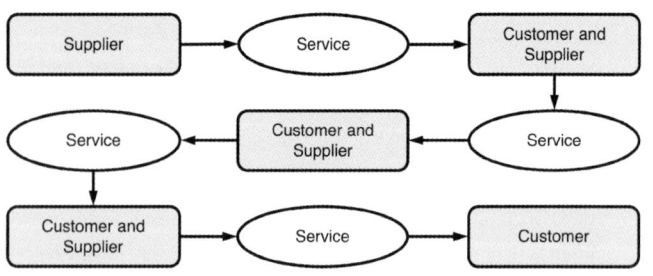

FIGURE 10

The chain of service organizations with customer and supplier roles

In the context of IT services, there is typically a chain of external service providers, internal IT functions, and internal or external end users. The IT function, therefore, fulfills the roles of service provider and service consumer. When the organization provides digital business services, the IT function is often an integrated part of business operations. These two situations are illustrated in Figure 11.

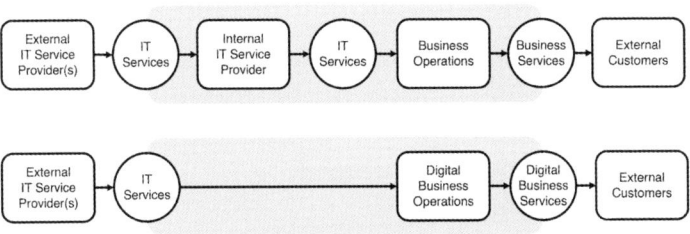

FIGURE 11

Two IT service chains

3.6.2 Experience

Experience is a set of emotions, feelings, and judgments that result from sensory perception while living through an event:

– Emotions are sensory expressions of feelings. They manifest themselves as physiological reactions, behavioral expressions, and judgments.
– Feelings are mental experiences that are related to, but independent of, what evoked them.
– Judgments are critical evaluations of events and people. They are based on the capacity to recognize relationships and draw conclusions from evidence.

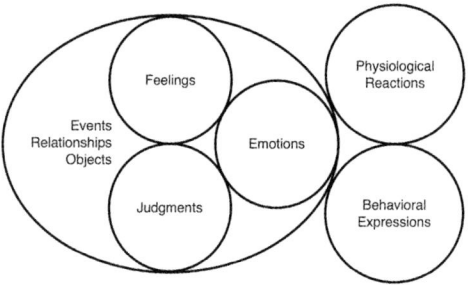

FIGURE 12

The anatomy of perception of events, relationships, and objects

Another meaning of experience is the knowledge from having lived through events. The distinction between the two meanings is usually clear from the context:
- Events are both individual moments and sets of related moments. For example, contact with the service desk is one of many moments that occur during the repair of a laptop.
- Experiences that occur "in-time" during each of these individual moments also contribute to the experience of the set of moments that evolves "over-time." In case of the laptop repair example, there will be an over-time experience of the specific laptop repair that, in turn, contributes to an over-time experience of the general relationship with the service provider.
- Each actor experiences a service differently, and each experience differs for each person.
- Each experience influences the provider-consumer relationship, with an essential role for trust in the provider's intentions, integrity, benevolence, and "technical" abilities in relevant domains, and their reciprocal trust.

- People's experience contributes to their desire for emotional well-being, so experience is a significant consideration in designing and executing human-centric services.

3.6.3 Experience Management

The commonly used definition of Experience Management (XM) in the marketplace is: The discipline of designing, measuring and improving the experiences provided to customers, employees, and other stakeholders. In the context of XLA, XM is defined as a set of activities that achieves better experience and greater business impact for both service consumer and service provider by driving and improving collaboration.

XM in the context of XLA includes:
- Agreeing on desired outcomes (human experience and business impact) with appropriate metrics and indicators.
- Monitoring the technology (O-data) and surveying how customers, employees, and other stakeholders experience services and products (X-data).
- Evaluating the data and discussing, defining, and initiating data-driven initiatives to improve customer experiences (touchpoints, service processes, product benefits).

The XLA Practice Areas define the scope of XM.

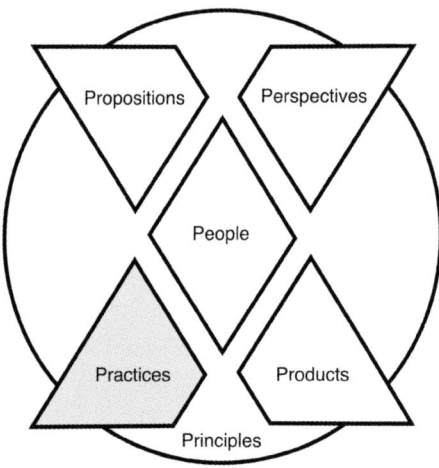

FIGURE 13

The XLA Practice Areas

3.6.4 Xperience Level Agreement (XLA)

An XLA is an outcome-oriented document. It is a measurable and verifiable agreement between the IT provider and the customer with respect to collaboration, experience, and business impact (the three XLA value drivers), see Figure 14.

Note the distinction between "XLA" and "an XLA". XLA without a preposition is used to denote Experience Management based on XLAs. For example: "We have adopted XLA." In this context, XLA is the concept of consensus between IT service provider and consumer regarding the desired human experience and business impact.

3. IT Service Experience and its Management

As described above, experience is the set of emotions, feelings, and judgments that result from sensory perception while living through an event.

Business impact is the tangible effect of IT on the business. The application of IT results in a change to the organization's resources in the broadest sense of the word. These are not only financial resources but also, for example, valuable knowledge and capabilities. IT can also affect the organization's products and services, and intangible resources such as reputation and goodwill.

Collaboration is the act of working with someone else in order to achieve something. It is the interpersonal part of service interactions. In IT service interactions, people also work with technology, for example when a service consumer uses the service provider's website. Technology-technology interactions can also be part of IT services.

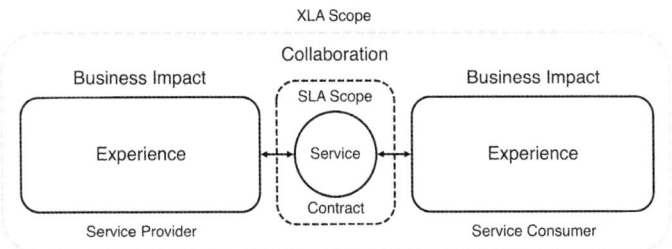

FIGURE 14

The role of the three XLA value drivers (Collaboration, Experience and Business impact) in service interactions

Collaboration is the only value driver that can be influenced directly by human intervention. Business impact and experience are the results of collaboration. Collaboration is, by definition, something that both provider and consumer are involved in at the same time. Both parties undergo business impact and experience from their own perspectives: there is business impact, consumer experience and provider experience for both parties.

Business impact is the tangible economic impact of the failure and success of IT on the business. It is influenced directly by collaboration and indirectly by experience because experience influences collaboration. Although business impact can be measured objectively, it is experienced subjectively: the same bottom-line results may be acceptable for one person but not for another. Experience is therefore not restricted to how the collaboration is experienced.

An XLA can manifest itself as:
- As an integral part of an SLA.
- As an addition to an SLA.
- As a separate document that overrides an SLA.

Most Service Level Agreements (SLAs) comprise the following parts:
1. **Context:**
- The contract that refers to the SLA
- Procedures for the use of services (often as a separate but related document)
2. **Scope:**
- A list and description of the (standard or custom) services to be provided

3. **Service quality levels, metrics, and conditions (generic or per service):**
   – Functionality, e.g., operation according to specifications
   – Availability, e.g., service window, percentage available, duration of outages, hours of support
   – Performance, e.g., reaction time and solution time for service requests
   – Security, e.g., effectiveness of prevention of social engineering attacks on systems, time to restore backed-up data
4. **Process:**
   – Roles and responsibilities
   – Monitoring
   – Reporting
   – Improvement

An XLA can be an integral part of an SLA, an addition to an SLA, or a separate document that overrides an SLA. The table below shows how an SLA as described above can be enhanced with XLA aspects (right) that make a more explicit connection with the desired business impact of the services (in part 1), the desired experience (in part 3), and the desired collaboration (in part 4).

Table of SLA contents	Table of XLA contents
Context	

– The contract that refers to the SLA
– Procedures for the use of services (often as a separate but related document)
	– Contribution of this XLA to the digital or ICT strategy
	  - Digital or ICT strategy
	  - Goal of this XLA concerning the digital or ICT strategy
	– Customer organization's core values
	  - Description of the core values

Scope	
– A list and description of the (standard or custom) services to be provided	
Service quality levels, metrics, and conditions (generic or per service)	

– SLA KPIs:
  - Functionality, e.g., operation according to specifications
  - Availability, e.g., service window, percentage available, duration of outages, hours of support
  - Performance, e.g., reaction time and solution time for service requests
  - Security, e.g., effectiveness of prevention of social engineering attacks on systems, time to restore backed-up data
	– XLA XIs:
	  - XLA XIs and their contribution to the core values

Table of SLA contents	Table of XLA contents
Process	

- Roles and responsibilities
- Monitoring
- Reporting
- Improvement
	- Monitoring:
	  - Method of measuring the XLA XIs
	  - Procedure for dealing with the measurements
	- Improvement:
	  - Procedure for dealing with SLAs that conflict with the XLA KPIs
	  - Procedure for using the measurements for continuous improvement
	  - Scheme for a bonus system that stimulates continuous improvement

3.6.5 Metrics

In modern IT Service Management, three types of metrics are essential: goals, indicators, and data.

1. **Goals:** XLA goals are the desired conditions of each of the three XLA value drivers and are derived from the organization's overall ambition and its ambition for each of its services.
   For example: the XLA goal of "quick and easy service" contributes to the organization's ambition of having happy customers.
2. **Indicators:** Key Performance Indicators (KPI) define the O-data, while Experience Indicators (XI) define the X-data.
   For example: that Customer Effort Score (CES) is a good indicator of achievement of the XLA goal "quick and easy service."
3. **Data:** O-data (Operational data) are measurements of objective performance of IT systems, processes, and service interactions, while X-data (Experience data) are measurements of the IT service

user's subjective experience. In both cases, there are captured data and processed data.

For example: the captured CES that a single customer reports, and, after processing, the calculated average of all captured CES per month.

A car analogy clarifies the difference between an XI and X-data: the indicator is speed, the captured data is currently 55 km/hour, and the processed data is an average of 32 km/h since the last refueling.

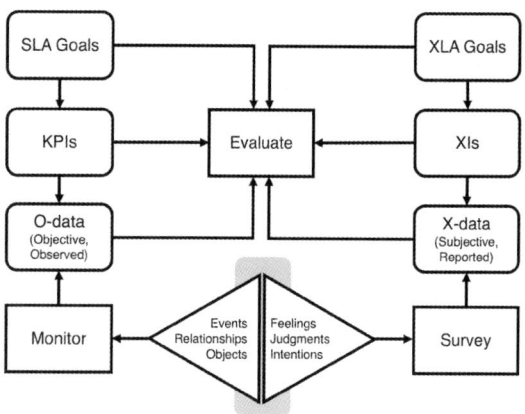

FIGURE 15

Relationships between key XLA concepts

In addition to the usual Service Management metrics that track the performance of devices, networks, applications, and processes, organizations that practice Experience Management collect data about what users think and how they feel about their interactions with information systems and the people who are involved in providing IT services. These subjective sentiment data that are collected by surveys are called X-data. X-data complements the observed and objective data (O-data) about devices, networks, applications, and processes.

Some algorithms represent hypothesized correlations between X-data and O-data. These algorithms help to predict the user sentiment that results from a certain level of technical performance. The prediction is used to initiate measures that prevent or at least reduce the need for users to contact the service desk. More significantly, it keeps the service and its output at a level that enables the Desired Outcome to be achieved.

The data and algorithms are part of a so-called objectives cascade that ensures their alignment with the organization's strategic objectives.

No Red Mondays

In the Netherlands, temporary employment agencies pay their employees weekly. Every Monday afternoon, the timesheets of the previous week are processed. When outsourcing salary payments, Monday afternoon is "the moment of truth." That moment is critical for User Experience. KPIs rarely take defining moments for User Experience into account. Applying the XLA approach, a Dutch temp agency introduced the concept of "Red Monday": if there are any disruptions for longer than fifteen minutes, that Monday is graded as "red." "No Red Mondays" became the most important indicator in the outsourcing relationship between the temping agency and payroll processing company. When there were zero Red Mondays in a month, this was celebrated to increase motivation among employees. Working with this KPI also created better satisfaction among top management.

4

Organization of IT Service Experience Management

So, what needs to be in place? The previous chapter described the increasingly higher demands people place on how they feel about providing and consuming IT services and how a better IT service experience has a positive business impact. This chapter describes the organizational structure and other resources that are needed to adopt and practice IT service Experience Management as an integrated part of IT service management.

The chapter covers:
- IT Service Management before adoption of Experience Management.
- How the adoption of Experience Management affects the IT Service Management operating model.
- Definitions and descriptions of key XLA concepts that are covered in this chapter.

4.1 IT Service Management Before Adoption of Experience Management

Most organizations that decide to adopt Experience Management do not start with a blank slate. They are either IT service providers or IT service consumers, or both, and have organized the IT management services accordingly. There are various kinds of organizations that manage the provision or consumption of IT services:

- An organization's IT department or function not only provides IT services to their internal or external users. They also consume IT services from external IT service providers.
- A business function will be an IT service consumer unless they offer digital products and services, in which case they will be both consumer and provider.
- A managed IT service provider or another kind of external IT service provider not only provides services but, just like the IT department, also consumes IT services from other parties.

These organizations all have the desire to improve the value derived from IT services and the belief that investment in IT service experience and its business impact fosters more meaningful, rewarding, and productive work. The bottom line is that they want happier people and better business.

The people who are concerned about the quality of IT services will most likely have been experimenting with various improvements within their current operating model. In other words, within the current set of people, resources, suppliers, and activities with which they create and provide their value propositions. Most IT Service Management organizations have adopted and adapted a framework such as ITIL® or

4. Organization of IT Service Experience Management

IT4ITTM as the basis for their operating model. Figure 16 illustrates such a high-level operating model for IT service management.

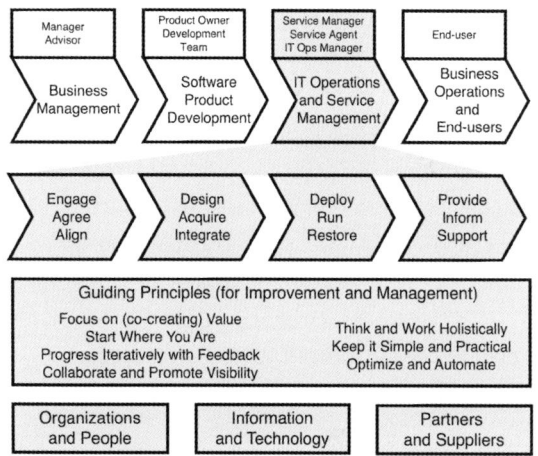

FIGURE 16

An IT service management operating model

In the broader value chain at the top of Figure 16, IT Service Management is positioned between business management, software product development (and external service providers), IT operations, and business operations.

The figure illustrates (from top to bottom) the core elements of the IT service management operating model:
− Roles, in particular, business manager, service manager, service agent, and end-user

- Capabilities and processes, in particular for agreement, design, acquisition, and integration deployment, delivery and support
- Guiding principles for improvement and management
- Internal and external resources

This is the starting point for the adoption of Experience Management: the familiar IT service management operating model. People will have conducted experiments with limited success within their current operating model and there is now a belief that structural change will enable significant progress with Experience Management.

4.2 IT Service Management after Adoption of Experience Management

4.2.1 Task Force

Typically, the adoption of XM starts with a pilot incorporating just a few services in order to keep things manageable. The initiative is usually driven by the individual manager who has "sold" the initiative to their managerial board and to their team. Crucially, there is funding to allocate people and resources to start the Experience Management Journey. The initial team is referred to as the Task Force. Their task is twofold: to improve the value of the IT services in scope, and to establish a way of working that can be adopted on a larger scale.

4.2.2 Experience Management Office

Once XM has become business-as-usual, the Task Force transfers its responsibilities to a permanent Experience Management Office (XMO) that gradually expands the scope to improve and manage more IT services from an Experience Management perspective. The Task Force is then disbanded, although some of its members may assume roles in the XMO. These roles can be temporary (for the sake of continuity of knowledge) or permanent. It is important to note that both the Task Force and the XMO are organizational functions rather than distinct units. There will be a dedicated core and co-workers from other functions that have (part-time) Experience Management roles. One of the key tasks of the XMO is to coordinate Experience Management activities across the broader organization.

The introduction of the Task Force is the first change to the existing operating model. Other changes are described below.

4.2.3 XLA Mindset

The XLA Mindset is the conviction that it is possible to let go of old belief systems and traditional managerial reflexes. This is a prerequisite for adopting a new way of working based on XLA. Convictions are firmly held beliefs. It would be immoral to impose such beliefs on employees, so employees must be selected with the XLA Mindset in mind. Suitable candidates already have this conviction, or they are open to adopting it.

4.2.4 XLA Skillset

An XLA training program is introduced and people are trained, for example in the value of empathy and how to apply it. This results in a team or organization with people who have the right skills to execute Experience Management: the XLA Skillset. Formal structures for knowledge-sharing are introduced, and informal networks are fostered. Informal networks are important because service work is intrinsically unpredictable. Because it is impossible to have all the required knowledge available beforehand, it is effective to know who might have that knowledge and to approach them as the need occurs. This is in addition to knowledge available outside of the organization.

4.2.5 XLA Toolset
In order to measure and analyze IT service experience, data-oriented tools are acquired and deployed. This is a significant part of the XLA Toolset. See Section 4.3 Products for more about the XLA Toolset.

4.2.6 XLA Template
New requirements are introduced for IT service offerings and agreements. This helps to extend the focus from the "technical" service output to include its business impact and how it is experienced by both service consumer and provider. There is an XLA Template available from the XLA Consortium that is used to extend the scope of existing Service Level Agreements.

4.2.7 Personas
People all have their own needs, wishes, and expectations. They use IT in different ways, times, and places. This is a major challenge for service providers. How to make sure that everyone gets what they need, desire, and expect? Start by identifying groups of end users that share the same values and needs. These groups of somewhat similar end users are called "personas."

Personas are logical groups of people based on their IT preferences, IT characteristics, lifestyles, or roles in an organization. It is key to understand what motivates and frustrates end users, and what is of utmost importance to them. Often, personas are visualized as posters.

The poster will usually feature a photo or drawing of a person surrounded by a name, a quote, and their demographic and psychographic characteristics. There will also be practices for product development and service design in which the personas are used.

To correctly identify personas, there has to be an understanding of the role IT plays in people's daily work before, during, and after using the service. For which tasks and processes is the persona most dependent on IT? Which devices and functionalities do they use most often? For which work have they hired the service? What are the moments of truth when IT really makes the difference, and what are the personas' digital skills and educational background? To get all these questions answered, people should be interviewed so that personas can be created based on common preferences and characteristics. Then visualize and describe the persona in a persona template. The result will likely be surprising. As Peter Drucker said in the 1960s: "The customer rarely buys what the company thinks it sells him."

4.2.8 Experience Management Journey
The Experience Management Journey is used as an approach to structure adoption and improvement of XM. It is described in detail in Section 5.2.

4.2.9 Experience Management
Experience Management activities are defined in high-level value streams and value stream steps that are integrated or closely aligned with existing IT Service Management value streams. This is described in more detail in Sub-section 3.6.3.

4.2.10 XLA Practices

XLA Practices are introduced to support specific parts of XM and the Experience Management Journey. For some organizations, specific XLA Practices are safe and repetitive ceremonies for celebration, trauma or other intense moments. In these cases, the XLA Practice is referred to as an XLA Ritual.

Chef's Table is an example of an XLA Practice (and often XLA Ritual) that ensures that the right stakeholders are involved and engaged. "Chef's Table" is a metaphor for the table in or overlooking the kitchen of a restaurant. In the XLA context, it is critical to ask the question: are the right people sitting at the table? Stakeholder maps identify and categorize stakeholders according to their "power to influence" and their "level of interest" in the outcome of the desired change.

The map is a two-by-two grid with the "actively engaged" stakeholders placed top right. Such maps are essential but probably aren't enough. Too often, people believe that if they add enough benefits from innovation and push ideas from the IT organization or department harder, people will eventually say "yes." Yet people often forget to overcome hidden friction because they don't listen and understand how the stakeholders feel.

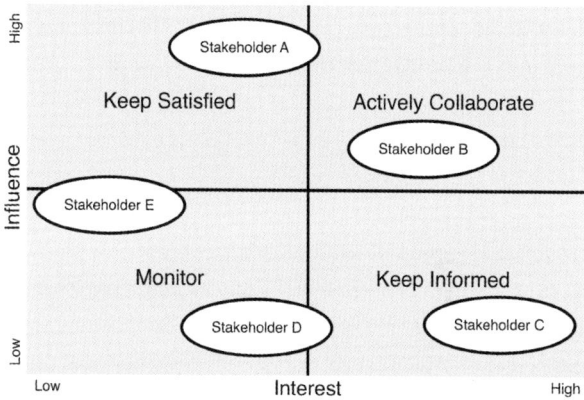

FIGURE 17

Stakeholder map

That's why XLA addresses the next level of stakeholder mapping to engage with the Chef's Table. Why? Power is also about informal power, and interest is also about resistance to change. The word "frenemy" is a figure of speech combining the words friend and enemy. To make change work, the organization must "keep its friends close and its enemies even closer." Leaders also have to lead, direct, or achieve without formal power.

Corporate structures drive formal power. Informal power stems from the relationships that people build and the respect they earn from others. It's not only the traditional authorities and the ones with high levels of interest in success that need a seat at the Chef's Table.

In summary, these are the kind of changes to the operating model that are needed to adopt Experience Management. They are introduced and improved over time. The changed parts of the operating model vary in "maturity" depending on the requirements of the specific IT services, and on the ability of the Task Force or XMO to introduce and improve them. Chapter 5 describes how these changes are made.

4.3 Key XLA Concepts

This section defines and describes the key concepts for the IT Service Management operating model. It also explains how these XLA concepts are related to each other. These concepts are listed below within the relevant elements of the XLA 6P Framework, see Figure 18:

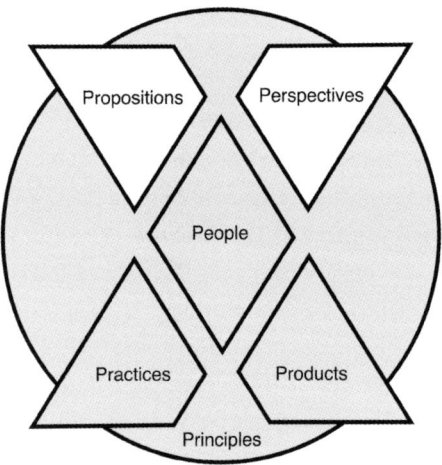

FIGURE 18

Relevant elements of the XLA 6P Framework

4. Organization of IT Service Experience Management

- **Principles:**
  - **XLA Principles:** beliefs that guide people in their decision-making in specific areas.
- **People:**
  - **XLA Mindset:** the conviction that it is possible to let go of old belief systems and traditional managerial reflexes to adopt the new way of working with XLA.
  - **XLA Skillset:** a set of skills needed to implement and execute new thinking from XLA Mindset.
  - **Task Force:** a temporary team that embraces and practices Experience Management until responsibility is transferred to an Experience Management Office.
  - **Experience Management Office (XMO):** a central and permanent function of an organization that embraces and practices Experience Management.
  - **XMO roles:** dedicated and part-time roles for the execution of the Experience Management Journey and Experience Management.
- **Practices:**
  - **XLA Practices:** sets of loosely defined activities that transform inputs into outputs in the context of a specific XLA practice area.
  - **XLA Rituals:** XLA practices that are safe and repetitive ceremonies for celebration, trauma or other intense moments.
  - **Experience Management Journey:** an approach for embedding Experience Management into the current operating model and continuously improving it.
- **Products:**
  - **XLA Toolset:** a set of tools needed to get a sufficient understanding of, and to focus management efforts on, collaboration,

experience, and business impact. It often includes software applications. These include tools for:
- IT service management
- Digital Experience Monitoring (DEM)
- Digital Customer Experience (DCX)
- Digital Employee Experience (DEX)

4.3.1 XLA Principles

Principles are beliefs that guide people in their decision-making. They fulfill various functions. They can govern activities by setting boundaries. Principles can also enable activities by giving people direction while allowing them to decide upon the best way of achieving the desired results. They can be used as scaffolding or guardrails that guide relatively inexperienced practitioners but can be disregarded by more experienced practitioners who are encouraged to exercise their professional judgement. As such, XLA Principles complement XLA Practices. XLA Principles are used while following XLA Practices to choose the best way of executing XLA Practices within the given context. In complex systems where behavior is inherently unpredictable, it is better to be guided by principles than to rigidly follow pre-determined processes.

Examples:
- People over technology.
- Perception over facts.
- Direction over destination.
- XLA over SLA (goal over means).

- Accuracy over precision.
- Outside-in over inside-out.
- The impact of IT on people and their business defines the value.
- Consistency in Experience Management is better than customer delight.
- The mindset for change is positive and performance driven.
- Empowered and intrinsically motivated people drive and lift performance.
- Collaboration only works when all parties benefit and are empathetic and confident.

4.3.2 Mindset, Skillset, and Toolset

These are the key success factors for an organization. People adopt a Mindset and develop a Skillset. The organization provides people with a data-oriented Toolset that helps them to understand and manage customer experience, business impact, and collaboration.

The XLA Mindset is the conviction that it is possible to let go of old belief systems and traditional managerial reflexes to adopt the new way of working with XLA.

The XLA Skillset is a set of skills needed to implement and execute new thinking from XLA Mindset.

The XLA Toolset is a set of tools needed to get a sufficient understanding of, and to focus management efforts on, collaboration, experience, and business impact. It often includes software applications.

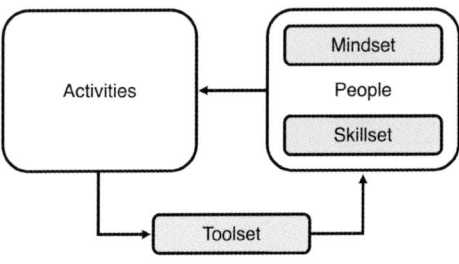

FIGURE 19

Mindset, Skillset, and Toolset

4.3.3 Task Force

A Task Force is a temporary team that embraces and practices Experience Management. It implements the key success factors mentioned above. The goal of a Task Force is to rapidly improve collaboration that results in better experience and greater business impact for all stakeholders, both inside and outside the organization. It remains in effect until Experience Management becomes business-as-usual with a roadmap, processes, and governance (evaluate, direct, monitor) in place. At that point, responsibility is transferred to an XMO. For continuity, Task Force members may staff the XMO, at least for its initial period of operation.

4.3.4 Experience Management Office (XMO)

An Experience Management Office (XMO) is a central and permanent function of an organization that embraces and practices Experience Management. The goal of an XMO is to continuously improve experience and collaboration that generates business impact, both inside and outside the organization. In large organizations, there may be several departmental XMOs that are coordinated by a central XMO.

As a function rather than a discrete organizational unit, the XMO is spread across the organization. While there are people who execute "pure" Experience Management roles, some existing roles such as IT service managers and IT service desk agents are tasked with additional Experience Management responsibilities. Typical XMO roles are:

- **Facilitator.** A facilitator is a coach to innovative, productive group thinking who works with a breed of core concepts for XM (like design thinking, Agile practices, ITIL4, and XLA) to make things happen within the organization and its ecosystem.
- **Experience architect.** An architect in XM is involved in Business-IT challenges, value propositions, and performance criteria. They inform, support, and direct UX designers, developers, delivery and service managers, tribe leaders, and teams (e.g., key-value indicators based on UX data).
- **ITSM liaison.** An ITSM liaison supports the development and continual improvement of ITSM processes and tools by providing factual information about how users (employees and customers) are experiencing products, processes, and projects.
- **Experience engineer.** An experience engineer is responsible for understanding user behaviors before and during the development of a product, project, or process by identifying user needs and pain points through gathering research, conducting interviews and focus groups, running A/B tests, organizing releasing qualitative and quantitative feedback processes, and collecting data. An experience engineer can play a role within a product team.
- **Tool master.** A tool master controls all tools and platforms in order to monitor, measure, integrate, and collect User Experience (ITSM, DEM/DEX/EUEM, data lakes, and AI).

- **Data curator.** A data curator takes care of the organization's metadata for Experience Management. Up-to-date and managerial knowledge about structured and unstructured datasets, databases, and the use of AI (NLP, ML, emotional AI) is critical.
- **Data scientist.** A data scientist creates value by fetching, automating, analyzing patterns, and presenting statistical information from various sources to improve IT's impact on business performance and user experience.
- **Performance manager.** A performance manager is responsible for the design and governance (including the reporting on key-value indicators for sprints, XIs for XLAs, and relevant KPIs) for external and internal parties involved in value streams and ecosystems.

There are parallels with other "offices" such as the Project Management Office. Both are tasked with maintaining standards for their particular area and are the sources of documentation, guidance, and metrics.

4. Organization of IT Service Experience Management

Task Force	XMO
Both the Task Force and XMO embrace and practice Experience Management which aims to improve collaboration that enhances experience and generates business impact for all stakeholders both inside and outside an organization.	
Temporary (multi-year) team.	Central and permanent function of an organization.
Mission is to improve rapidly.	Mission is to improve continuously.
Temporary funded (fact-based).	Permanently funded through a central organization (faith-based).
Remains in effect until Experience Management becomes business-as-usual with a roadmap, processes, and governance in place. At that point, responsibility is transferred to an XMO.	Takes over ownership from Task Force. In large organizations, there may be several departmental XMOs that are coordinated by a central XMO.

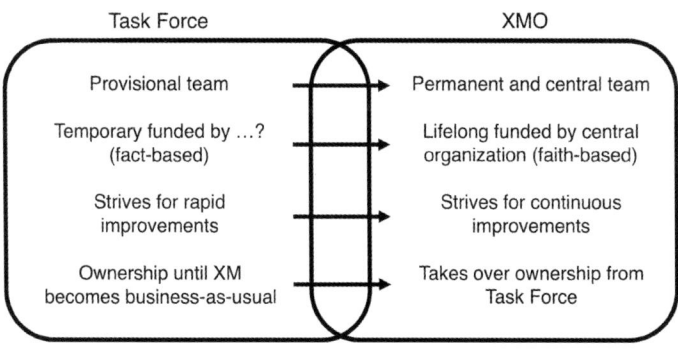

FIGURE 20

Taskforce vs. XMO

4.3.5 XLA Practices

An XLA Practice is a set of activities that transforms inputs into outputs; XLA Practices can fulfill value stream steps. Practices are similar to processes, that also transform inputs into outputs, but they are less tightly defined. XLA Practices are used as "building blocks" in the context of the XLA Practice Areas. Most XLA Practices support a specific XLA Practice Area but the more generic XLA Practices support more than one XLA Practice Area.

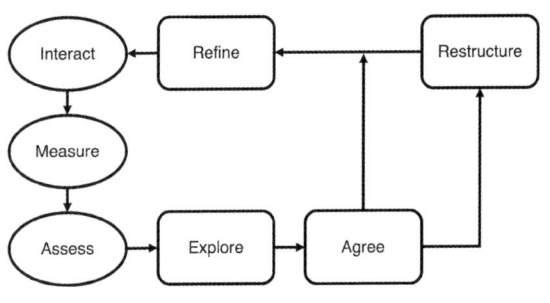

FIGURE 21

The XLA Practice Areas

The XLA Practices do not cover all of the XLA Practice Areas. They offer solutions such as workshops that help fulfill specific parts of the XLA Practice Areas.

4.3.6 XLA Rituals

An XLA Ritual is a safe and repetitive ceremony for celebration, trauma or other intense moment. XLA Rituals are XLA Practices that have a ceremonial significance for the organization in question. This may change over time and differ from what other organizations regard as rituals.

Most contracting parties that commit to XLA want the XLA to be an enforceable, mutually beneficial agreement. However, more than a signed contract is needed to make XLA work. It is vital to have rituals that remind the parties of their shared values and goals so that they honor the contract. For example, a ritual could manifest itself as a periodic meeting between stakeholders in which they are able to openly share and reflect on how they work together, what they are actually getting out of the relationship, and what they would like to get out of it.

KPI Stress Test

An example of an XLA Ritual is the KPI Stress Test. The purpose of KPIs is to trigger positive outcomes. When this doesn't happen, the tendency is to add new KPIs to the contracting between IT provider and customer. This complicates the process more and it is easy to lose sight of what will actually create positive outcomes in the jungle of KPIs. By "stress testing" the current KPIs, the side-effects of KPIs can be cross-checked: are they doing more harm than good? As Marylin Strathern paraphrased Goodhart's Law: "When a measure becomes a target, it ceases to be a good measure." The goal of stress testing is to determine the effectiveness of a system. Is the organization actually working with Key Performance Indicators, or are they just using Killers of Potential Innovation?

KPIs can be tested against perverse incentives (undesirable behavior), negative impact (unwanted outcomes), and incompatibility (unintended negative coherence).

1. **Perverse incentives.** Which KPIs are perverse incentives that cause undesirable human behavior due to penalties or shame?

2. **Negative impact.** Which KPIs harm something more essential and therefore cause undesirable outcomes for the business and the customers?
3. **Incompatibility.** Which KPIs conflict with other KPIs and "short circuit" effective performance management?

A ritual to identify perverse incentives is Cheat! This entails asking people which KPIs have been reported "green" on dashboards but were actually a waste of time or even counterproductive. The discussion can be opened with the provocative question of how people "game" the system to achieve the KPI. Incompatible KPIs can be identified with the Awkward! ritual. This is based on the Golden Raspberry Awards for the worst movie. Introduce a ritual to nominate incompatible KPIs and shred the worst entry.

4.3.7 Xperience Management Journey

The Experience Management Journey is an approach for embedding XM into the current operating model and continuously improving it. Both the Task Force and the XMO use the Experience Management Journey. The Task Force uses the Experience Management Journey for the introduction of XM and the initial change to the organization. The XMO uses the Experience Management Journey to continuously improve the XMO and other parts of the organization involved in XM, and to expand its scope of IT services. This five-phase approach is described in Chapter 5.

5

Transformation of the IT Service Management Organization

How to get there? The previous chapter described the organizational structure and other resources that are needed to adopt and practice IT service experience management as an integrated part of IT Service Management. This chapter describes an approach for adopting IT service experience management and embedding it into IT Service Management activities.

The chapter covers:
- How to tackle the inevitable resistance encountered when adopting Experience Management in an organization.
- Using the Experience Management Journey to adopt and improve Experience Management.
- The long-term perspective for Experience Management.
- Definitions and descriptions of key XLA concepts that are covered in this chapter.

5.1 Resistance

Spoiler alert: introducing Experience Management in an organization will not go without a decent amount of resistance. SLA thinking is persistent in IT Service Management. "We execute contracts, we don't get rewards for pleasing customers." "We don't have time to do this, we are too busy." "It's not our fault, it's the account manager's problem." "We can't improve this; it is what it is." "I'm getting tired of this stuff, you sound like my partner."

People who introduce XLA in their organization may feel as if the odds are stacked against them. Maybe some of their colleagues will embrace XLA from the beginning, but probably quite a few will give them a hard time. Changing a dominant belief system takes time – and balls.

5.1.1 Stuck in SLA-thinking

Service Level Agreements are essential for managing contractual obligations. A negative side-effect of "overthinking SLAs" is maxing out the relationship between suppliers and customers: reaching a point where no more improvement, profit, or benefit occurs. SLAs drive mediocre services, not a "good enough" Customer Experience. SLAs are often used and eventually abused to prove that the customer should be happy: "We hit all the contractual metrics, so stop complaining."

The performance perspective is binary: either the service level targets are met, or they are not. From a delivery perspective, SLAs are clear: they must be fulfilled. It's a catch-22, an inescapable paradoxical situation: the service level report metrics are met but the customer is not satisfied. IT makes or breaks the core business of most organizations, from their daily operations to fueling their next business model.

Mechanisms that ensure that customers get what they want, or need are almost non-existent in an SLA-driven world. Yet, many people in IT are stuck in SLA-thinking.

5.1.2 Yin and Yang

When introducing XLA in an organization, it can be helpful to understand the concept of confirmation bias. Confirmation bias is the human tendency to process information in a manner that confirms our prior convictions, and disregards information that does not conform to what people already believe to be true. People prefer to interpret new information as consistent with their existing beliefs. When people encounter other beliefs and objective evidence contradicting these existing beliefs, they claim that the new information must be wrong. They try to reframe that information, distance themselves from it, and even discredit it.

Confirmation bias is one of the biggest hurdles on the road to introducing XLA. How to deal with challenging an entire belief system that is based on SLA? The first step is to highlight SLAs' flaws and shortcomings. Often, people cannot rethink their beliefs until they understand something is missing from their current belief system. Evoke empathy and invite people to rethink their views by showing what is missing. The persistent belief that SLAs are the "only truth" is based on one interpretation of reality. It is critical to present an addition to that reality. SLA and XLA are complementary forces, they are two realities that can exist at the same time. Introducing XLA as the yang to SLA's yin will allow people to accept the change to XLA.

5.1.3 Stories Matter

When confronted with people who strongly believe in processes first, it is more effective to focus on emotions than facts. When one person listens to another person's story, they are not only perceiving the speaker's verbal and non-verbal communication. Our brain also tries to synchronize. At the beginning of listening to another person's story, the listener's brain activity is slightly delayed: the listener hears the content first. But then, the listener's brain activity will follow and predict the speaker's brain.

By eliciting emotion, people can change perceptions. When storytellers can evoke emotion, they are somewhat in control of that person's state of mind. A captivating rhetorical style is not only about the words; it's about brains synchronizing. With great, compelling speeches, like Kennedy's famous moon speech or Martin Luther King's "I have a dream", the listener's brain started preceding the storyteller's brain activity because the listener's mind was predicting what the storyteller would say. The essential ingredient in adopting XLA in an all-SLA belief system is sharing stories about actual customer cases with real people directly or indirectly impacted by IT services.

	Fit for Purpose	**Onboarding**
Purpose	Software expenditure per employee represents, on average, +25% of the total IT spend of companies. The value is too often intangible. F4P is a litmus test.	Poor onboarding is a significant cause of employee turnover, costing a company 100-300%% of the employee's salary in total. Onboarding is an IT-HR tandem.
Desired Outcome	Fit for Purpose (F4P) means that business applications must be good enough to do the job. Low F4P is needed to strip out waste based on the voice of the consumer.	When a new employee comes to work for the first day, they must be able to start working, rather than wait for IT or HR to sort things out.
Experience Indicator	Subjective feedback related to Fit for Purpose helps to prioritize (the backlog) and prevents throwing good money after bad in application Life Cycle Management.	"Welcome" to measure onboarding experience as a heartbeat during the first two months. Low scores trigger proactive support. Tracking for 24 months optional.
X + O Data	Correlation with O-data from IT Asset Management (ITAM) tools on software inventory tracking and DEM tools for non-functional application performance.	Correlation with O-data on timeliness of onboarding processes like registering new accounts and profiles to various systems in HR, IT, and probably Facilities.

FIGURE 22

XLA objectives cascade with examples

5.2 The Experience Management Journey

Chapter 4 described the changes to the IT Service Management operating model that enables it to extend its scope to the impact of IT services on people and their business. It stated that these changes are introduced and improved over time. The changed parts of the operating model vary in "maturity" depending on the requirements of the specific IT services, and on the ability of the Task Force or XMO to introduce and improve them. This chapter now describes how these changes are made by adopting and adapting the approach proposed in the Experience Management Journey.

5.2.1 Cyclical Approach

The Experience Management Journey is a cyclical approach for embedding XM into the current operating model and continuously improving it. It is initially executed by a temporary Task Force until an effective way of working has been established. Then it is transferred to a permanent Experience Management Office that gradually expands the scope to improve and manage more IT services from an Experience Management perspective.

5.2.2 Building, Running, and Improving the Shop

The Experience Management Journey is executed in parallel with Experience Management. XM is about "running the shop", while the Experience Management Journey is about initially "building the shop" and then "continuously improving the shop." There is, of course, close interdependence and interaction between XM and the Experience Management Journey. Feedback from XM is an important source of improvement initiatives that are executed in the Experience Management Journey, and these improvements result in changes to XM.

5.2.3 Five Interconnected Phases

The Experience Management Journey comprises five interconnected phases:

1. "Define" determines the scope of the Experience Management Journey, defining the organization's purpose and positioning; its commitments regarding service, collaboration, business impact, and experience; the current and desired perception and the consequences for core capabilities; the main economic driver; and a clear and compelling goal (Big Hairy Audacious Goal, BHAG).
2. "Discover" aims to clarify the existing situation and focuses on measuring the current experience, collaboration, and business impact.
3. "Dream" establishes what could be achieved, given the existing situation and the defined BHAG.
4. "Design" focuses on creating, improving, and renewing services and experiences in co-creation, optimizing collaboration, and providing guidelines for the realization of the XLA agreement and the Experience Management Office.
5. "Deliver" is about delivering, monitoring, and reporting better experience, enhanced collaboration, and improved services.

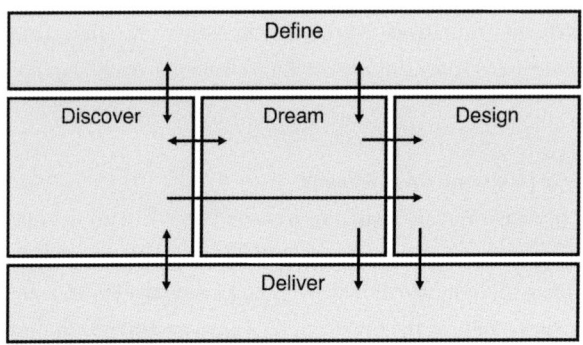

FIGURE 23

The five interconnected phases of the Xperience Management Journey

5.2.4 Stepping Stones

Rather than looking at the Experience Management Journey as a fixed sequence of steps, these five phases should be regarded as stepping stones that offer multiple entry points for improvement, depending on the nature of the improvement and the current improvement potential of the organization. At the very start of the journey, the phases will usually be followed in sequence. When Experience Management for a specific service is operational, however, the focus will be mainly on Deliver, with excursions to other phases, depending on the nature of the situation. Most improvements to operational services will be tackled in Design. When Define, Discover, and Dream are applied to operational services, it will usually be a question of reviewing and adjusting the initial choices rather than starting from scratch. When new services are added to the scope of Experience Management, the initial sequential journey may be repeated but more quickly, benefiting from the practical experience that was obtained from working with previous services.

5.3 The Long-term Perspective

5.3.1 Building the Plane While Flying It

So, are we there yet? Yes and no. You're there when you realize that "there" doesn't exist. The XLA Consortium is "building the plane while flying it." The emergent and evolving nature of XLA and Experience Management also applies within individual organizations. Because each person experiences service differently, and for each person, each experience differs, consequently the metrics, indicators, and measures should be continuously monitored against desired outcomes and improved as appropriate.

XLA is a never-ending story: even when the term is replaced by something else, it will live on in its offspring. Where will the XLA movement be in the future? It is hard to say. As David Bowie once said: "I don't know where I'm going from here, but I promise it won't be boring." Tech needs touch like yin needs yang. Emotional intelligence is a must-have in tech for digital product discovery and delivery. The IT industry needs more people "in tech", not acting like they are "from tech."

5.3.2 A Leap of Faith

We are on a mission to bridge separated worlds. In 2011, Marc Andreesen famously wrote a Wall Street Journal essay declaring that "software is eating the world." Five years later, the five most prominent companies in the world by market capitalization were all software companies. As technology becomes more and more pervasive across industries and functions, almost all large companies want to become tech-driven companies. The XLA Consortium hopes to make a modest contribution with XLA. Business impact, experience, and collaboration are three value drivers for XLA. Join us in growing the movement, sharing good practices, and seeking to inspire others to take a leap of faith.

5.3.3 The Rise and Fall of Experience Management

What goes up, must come down. Now that IT service experience management is on the upside of the hype cycle, it is good to contemplate its inevitable fall. But what could possibly go wrong with a movement that aims to benefit people's emotional well-being by applying empathy to how they experience IT services?

The same question could be asked of project management that emerged in the 1980s to get a better grip on the growth of the software development industry. Where did it end up? In a dictatorship with project managers imposing deliverables and deadlines that only gave the illusion of control. IT Service Management in the 1990s? Bureaucracy and theatre. Agile in the 2000s? Schisms and fundamentalism. DevOps in the 2010s? Elitism and new silos.

Back to Experience Management. In their enthusiasm to ensure that users and other stakeholders have a good experience, service providers could end up as melodramatic nannies who know what is good for the service recipients.

As always, it is a question of balance. In this case, while human empathy is essential, attention to procedural predictability and technical competence will keep experiential excesses in check. Long after the disillusioned experience evangelists have moved on to the next

5. Transformation of the IT Service Management Organization

shiny new thing, Experience Management will become an integral part of IT Service Management with the human touch.

5.4 Key XLA Concepts

This section defines and describes the key concepts for the IT Service Management operating model. It also explains how these XLA concepts are related to each other. These concepts are listed below within the relevant elements of the XLA 6P Framework:

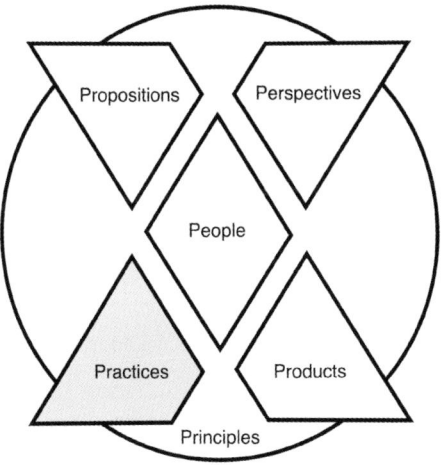

FIGURE 24

Relevant elements of the XLA 6P Framework

- **Practices:**
  - **Experience Management Journey:** an approach for embedding Experience Management into the current operating model and continuously improving it (described in Sub-section 4.3.5).
- **Practice Areas:**
  - The Experience Management Journey manifests itself mainly in the XLA Practice Areas Explore, Agree, and Modify with respect to the organizational function of Experience Management. The five phases are mapped to the XLA Practice Areas as follows:
    - Define corresponds with the XLA Practice Area Explore.
    - Discover corresponds with the XLA Practice Area Explore.
    - Dream corresponds with the XLA Practice Area Explore.
    - Design corresponds with the XLA Practice Area Agree.
    - Deliver corresponds with the XLA Practice Area Modify.

5.4.1 The Define Phase of the Experience Management Journey

Define determines the scope of the Experience Management Journey, specifying:

- The organization's purpose and positioning.
- The commitments regarding service, collaboration, business impact, and experience.
- The current and desired perception and the consequences for core capabilities.
- The primary economic driver that, combined with purpose and positioning, helps define a clear and compelling goal (Big Hairy Audacious Goal, or BHAG).

5.4.2 The Discover Phase of the Xperience Management Journey

Discover aims to clarify the existing situation and focuses on measuring the current:

- **Experience** in terms of:
  - Who the customer is.
  - How the service is currently experienced.
  - The services in scope.
  - The steps the customer goes through before, during, and after using the service.
  - The internal processes needed to deliver the service performance.
- **Collaboration** in terms of:
  - The positioning in the service chain.
  - The parties in the service chain involved in the in-scope services.
  - The stakeholders that must be involved.
- **Business impact** in terms of:
  - The IT services and the business processes that they support.
  - The moments of truth.
  - The commitment and engagement of the business owners.
  - The prioritization of investments.

5.4.3 The Dream phase of the Experience Management Journey

Dream establishes what could be achieved, given the existing situation and the defined BHAG, using:

- The Zone of Good Enough: the range of acceptable quality levels for experiences that are not intended to be exceptional. This sets concrete goals per organization and per service, both internally and externally, for experience, collaboration, and business impact.
- An Empathy Map to specify the desired experience with statements, thoughts, feelings, and behaviors.

- Jobs to be Done (JTBD) to help determine customer requirements and to make the ambition per service more practical.
- A gap analysis to clarify the difference between the current results and the desired results.
- Initiatives formulated on gaps and prioritized by improvement in experience, and the amount of investment required.
- A roadmap that shows all milestones and initiatives in one overview.

5.4.4 The Design Phase of the Experience Management Journey

Design focuses on:

- Creating, improving, and renewing services and experiences in co-creation, including establishing the required combination of X-data and O-data, and XIs that reflect the ambition per service, per persona.
- Optimizing collaboration.
- Providing guidelines for the realization of:
  - The XLA.
  - The Experience Management Office.

5.4.5 The Deliver Phase of the Experience Management Journey

Deliver is about actually delivering, monitoring, and reporting better experience, better collaboration, and improved services:

- A temporary and result-oriented Task Force is set up to deliver this experience, collaboration, and service initially. When Experience Management is business-as-usual, with a roadmap, processes, and governance (evaluate, direct, monitor) in place, responsibility is transferred to a permanent XMO.

- Governance ensures monitoring and control, resulting in continuous improvement.
- Good processes create a rhythm of planning, doing, reflecting, and then planning again.
- Tooling enables organizations to measure, drive and maximize business results by optimizing User Experience.
- Survey responses are collected and visualized in dashboards, allowing an answer to a subjective question such as "how satisfied are you with IT?" to be displayed and interpreted.

6

Glossary

Experience Management (such as 5-D Model of Experience Management Journey) while other terms are generic but of particular value for Experience Management (such as business requirements).

Many of the terms are mentioned in the "key XLA concepts" sections of Chapters 2, 3, 4 and 5. These are the main concepts in the XLA way of thinking. The list is alphabetical for ease of reference and the definition and description often refer to related terms (underscored). There are references to sources at the end of the glossary that have been used to define and inspire the terms.

5-D Model of Experience Management Journey – *Definition* A series of coordinated phases intended to drive organizational change from a positive mindset. – *Description* The 5-D model is originally derived from the 5-D Appreciative Inquiry model (or cycle) that consists of five D's: Define, Discover, Dream, Design, and Deliver. The 5-D model of Experience Management Journey does not need to be followed in a particular order. Depending on the context and situation, you may decide to go back or skip a phase. It aims to continuously improve collaboration, and in turn, improves experience and business impact.

ABC Analysis – *Definition* A method for assessing and understanding behavior. – *Description* Antecedents (A) are circumstances that precede but do not necessarily cause behavior. Behavior (B) is what a person is observed to be doing. Consequences (C) are circumstances that arise as a result of behavior and affect the probability that the behavior will reoccur.[I, II] The most important conclusion is that behavior is mainly determined by what happens after the behavior. Antecedents provoke behavior, but it is consequences that determine whether the behavior is repeated in the future or not.

Ambition – *Definition* A stated desire that can be fulfilled by the XLA value drivers. – *Description* In the context of Experience Management, there is an overarching ambition for the organization that is based on its core values, purpose, and strategy. There are also ambitions for individual services. In both cases, ambition is specific enough to be translated into XLA goals.

Analytical Competence Tool (ACT) – *Definition* An online assessment tool to assess behavioral competencies. – *Description* The results help assess what type of function fits well with the person's natural behavioral competencies.

6. Glossary

Application Performance Monitoring (APM) – *Definition* A type of monitoring software. *Description* Application performance monitoring software includes Digital Experience Monitoring (DEM), application discovery, tracing and diagnostics, and purpose-built artificial intelligence for IT operations.

BHAG (Big Hairy Audacious Goal) – *Definition* A clear and compelling target for an organization to strive for. – *Description* BHAGs are meant to shift the way of how business is done, the way an organization is perceived in the industry, and possibly even shift the industry itself. BHAGs are bigger, bolder, and more powerful than regular long-term goals.

Buddies and Butlers – *Definition* A human-centered support model to help end users adapt to technology-driven change. – *Description* Buddies help with acclimatization for a short period of time (hours to weeks). Butlers train and support buddies in the background and provide long-term support. Buddies are usually end users in the business with an affinity for technology.

Business Impact – *Definition* The tangible effect of IT on the business. – *Description* Traditional IT metrics like availability and network latency are too often mumbo jumbo for business stakeholders. "99-point-whatever-percentages" are meaningless when you don't know the actual impact. Business impact can be both financial and non-financial. Business impact is one of the three value drivers.

Business Impact Poster – *Definition* A graphical, visualized one-pager (preferably poster format) expressing the business impact of IT failures on day-to-day business. – *Description* Impact examples are lost revenue, user productivity loss, and rework costs. Designing a BIP requires co-creation between a service provider and the customer.

Business Requirements – *Definition* A representation of goals, objectives, and outcomes that describe why a change has been initiated and how success will be assessed. – *Description* Business requirements focus on the outcome that is required by the business and why this outcome is needed, rather than how to achieve it. [III]

Carrot and Stick – *Definition* A metaphor for rewards and punishments that can be used to encourage desired behavior. – *Description* The metaphor is derived from the idea that a donkey can either be motivated to walk by dangling a carrot in front of it or by hitting it with a stick.

Chef's Table – *Definition* An XLA practice that ensures that the right stakeholders are involved and engaged. – *Description* It is a mental model to engage the powerful, the apparently powerless, the involved and the somehow detached stakeholders. The Chef's Table is a metaphor for the table in or overlooking the kitchen of a restaurant that is in close contact with the chef.

Chief Empathy Officer – *Definition* An alternative interpretation of the job-title CEO. – *Description* Empathy is more than a nice-to-have skill for executives. It drives business growth by fostering stronger relationships. Empathic leaders lead with purpose, are honest and transparent, and make people feel valued.

Circle of Concern – *Definition* Things that the organization cares about but can't change. – *Description* Too much focus on these things causes anxiety, stress, and passivity. The circle of concern is the largest of three concentric circles: concern, influence, and control.

Circle of Control – *Definition* Things that the organization cares about and can change on its own. – *Description* The organization can be held accountable for the results in this area. The circle of control is the smallest of the three concentric circles of concern, influence, and control.

Circle of Influence – *Definition* Things that the organization can do something about, even when it can't change them alone.
Description By connecting and collaborating with others, the organization's circle of influence expands. The circle of influence is in the middle of the three concentric circles of concern, influence, and control.

Code of Conduct – *Definition* A document about desirable and undesirable behavior in order to improve collaboration.

Collaboration – *Definition* The act of working with someone else in order to achieve something. – *Description* In successful collaborations, there are constructive win-win situations and agreement about a common goal. Collaboration is one of the three value drivers of XLA.

Commitments – *Definition* Obligations regarding the characteristics and quality of services and the co-creation with customers.

Complete Waste of Time (CWOT) – *Definition* An XLA practice to address the bad use of time with humor. – *Description* What needs to be stopped because there's no point in it? CWOT helps to make a not-to-do list.

Comply and Lie – *Definition* Potential providers' behavior to meet knock-out contract criteria to win, even when the criteria can't be met or are irrelevant.

Continuous Improvement – *Definition* The ongoing process of making the organization more effective or efficient.

Convergent Thinking – *Definition* The process of taking focused action after having explored an issue more widely or deeply (divergent thinking). [IV]

Cool Wall – *Definition* The visualization of humorous brainstorming on the coolness of things. – *Description* The Cool Wall was a segment in the BBC TV program Top Gear to determine the coolness factor of cars. The presenters placed photos in four categories (from left to right): Seriously Uncool, Uncool, Cool, and Sub Zero.

Core Capability Matrix – *Definition* A map of desired and current expertise. – *Description* The matrix distinguishes between desirability and feasibility. It helps to plot which services have the most impact on experience and achieve the desired perception.

Customer – *Definition* The consumer of an internal or external provider's IT products or services that are responsible for the outcome. – *Description* A customer is not necessarily an end user.

Customer Delight – *Definition* A strong positive emotional customer reaction to deliberately exceeded expectations.

Customer Experience (CX) – *Definition* A customer's perception of the relationship and interactions with an IT organization. – *Description* CX of the relationship happens on a cumulative basis. Also see User Experience.

Customer Journey Map – *Definition* A visualization of the chronological steps and associated emotions a customer goes through before, during, and after the use of a service. – *Description* It also visualizes pain points and areas for improvements.

Customer Lifetime Value (CLV) – *Definition* The average customer's revenue is generated over their entire relationship with a company.

Customer Loyalty – *Definition* A customer's willingness to stay with a brand or an organization. – *Description* It is a manifestation of the customer's ongoing emotional relationship with a brand or an organization.

Customer Satisfaction Score – *Definition* A commonly used metric that tracks how satisfied customers are with an organization's products and/or services.

Customer Experience Management (CXM) – *Definition* Customer Experience Management (CXM) is the discipline of understanding customers and deploying insights for a customer-centric culture to improve satisfaction, loyalty, and advocacy. – *Description* DEM supports CXM.

Define – *Definition* This phase of the Experience Management Journey determines the scope.

Deliver – *Definition* This phase of the Experience Management Journey is about delivering, monitoring, and reporting better experience, collaboration, and improved services.

Design – *Definition* This phase of the Experience Management Journey focuses on creating or improving collaboration, experiences, and services.

Digital Experience Monitoring (DEM) – *Definition* Digital Experience Monitoring (DEM) is a discipline that monitors the availability, performance and quality of applications and all of its components and endpoints that may impact the end-user experience. – *Description* The end-user is anyone and everything (including external customers, partners, internal employees and digital agents) that interacts with a service.

DEM's purview spans endpoint devices, core infrastructure, applications, and business processes to enable a comprehensive view of the end-user experience and translate them into business outcomes.

DEM includes Real User Monitoring RUM), Endpoint Monitoring (EP), and Synthetic Transaction Monitoring (STM). [v]

Digital Employee Experience (DEX) – *Definition* Digital Employee Experience (DEX) is a discipline that focuses on the digital experience of employees (no customer/consumer perspective). – *Description* DEX has evolved from DEM. In addition to performance monitoring in DEM, DEX also incorporates organizational context data (location, roles, employee type, etc.) and gathers contextual employee sentiment (about the use and performance of technology). This data is used by analytics/ML engines to produce actionable insights.DEM supports DEX.

Discover – *Definition* This phase of the Experience Management Journey aims to clarify the existing situation in terms of collaboration, experience, and business impact.

Divergent Thinking – *Definition* The process of exploring an issue more widely or deeply before taking focused action (convergent thinking). [VI]

Double Diamond – *Definition* A design process model shaped as two diamonds, representing the problem zone and the solution zone. – *Description* Both zones are diamonds because each diamond represents divergent and convergent thinking in each zone. [VII]

Dream – *Definition* This phase of the Experience Management Journey is about the direction and ambition within the constraints of the existing situation.

Early Adopter – *Definition* An early customer of a company, product, or technology. – *Description* Early adopters come after the innovators but before the early majority, late majority, and laggards. [VIII]

Ease of Doing Business Value – *Definition* The third level within the Elements of Value Pyramid. – *Description* This level offers some operational elements such as increased productivity and availability, and it includes the first subjective elements such as improving relationships between parties.

Elements of Value Pyramid – *Definition* A set of 30 elements of value that address four kinds of customer needs: functional, emotional, life changing, and social impact. – *Description* The pyramid organizes forty distinct kinds of value, within five levels, that Service Providers may offer their customers. The most objective values are found at the base, and the higher the level, the more subjective and personal values it contains. [IX]

Emotions – *Definition* Sensory expressions of feelings that manifest themselves as physiological reactions, behavioral expressions, and cognitive decisions. [X]

Empath – *Definition* A person who absorbs the world's joys and stresses like an "emotional sponge". – *Description* Empaths sense and feel the emotions of others as if they're part of the other person's experience. In other words, someone else's pain and happiness become their own. Also see Empathy.

Empathic Organization – *Definition* The type of organization that cultivates the ability to understand employees, customers, partners, and their community's thoughts, feelings, motivations, and conditions from their respective points of view. – *Description* The leadership of these organizations creates a high level of belonging, safety, trust, and coherence.

Empathy – *Definition* The ability to relate to the feelings of others, but also to understand their thoughts, experiences or challenges. – *Description* Being empathic does not mean agreeing with someone. It just means understanding the situation. Someone with a lot of empathy is an empath. Also see Empath, sympathy and rational compassion.

Empathy Debrief – *Definition* A collaborative visualization tool to recap what is learned about the needs of a particular type of user. – *Description* The first debrief canvas is about negative feedback (from unpleasant to problematic) and the second debrief canvas is about positive feedback (from pleasant to awesome).

Employee Engagement (EE) – *Definition* Employees' emotional involvement in their employer's success. – *Description* Emotional engagement is related to employee satisfaction (whether people are satisfied with their work and the work environment) and employee experience (how people feel about critical moments and customer journeys like onboarding).

Employee Experience (EX) – *Definition* Employees' perceptions about their interactions and touchpoints with an employer, from onboarding to exit. – *Description* The digital workspace and other technology services are essential components of the Employee Experience.

Endpoint Monitoring (EP) – *Definition* The type of technology that provides visibility into end-user devices from a health and CI performance perspective. – *Description* Examples: Wifi signal strength, HDD failures, CPU, memory and disk utilization. EP solutions are often (wrongly) positioned as DEM solutions. [XI]

End User – *Definition* The individual consumer of an internal or external provider's IT products or services that are responsible for the outcome. Also see Customer.

Experience – *Definition* The set of emotions, feelings, and judgments that result from sensory perception while living through an event. [XII]

Experience Economy – *Definition* In an experience economy, it is the experience that determines economic value. Understanding this critical change in the fabric of the economy allows us to rethink connecting with customers and securing their loyalty. – *Description* The experience economy is the next economy following the agrarian economy, the industrial economy, and the service economy. [XIII]

Expert Bias – *Definition* The inability of a person who has mastered a skill or acquired knowledge to understand non-experts. – *Description* The problem with expertise is that it is harder to put yourself in the shoes of someone unfamiliar with that topic or skill. [XIV]

Experience Cross-Reference Matrix – *Definition* A grid of relationship between O-data and X-data for each service. – *Description* Joint analysis of O-data and X-data provides actionable insights to manage experience.

Experience Indicator (XI) – *Definition* An Experience Indicator (XI) is a metric that captures personal thoughts and feelings – *Description* The data on XIs is called X-data and should be curated and correlated with objective data for proactively managing customer, employee or other human experiences.

Experience Management (XM) – *Definition* A set of activities that achieves better experience and greater business impact by driving and improving collaboration. – *Description* It is a data-driven approach that combines operational measurements (O-data) and sentiment measurements (X-data), so it correlates output (technology focused) with outcome (human focused).

Experience Management Journey – *Definition* An approach for embedding Experience Management into the current operating model and continuously improving it.

Experience Management Office (XMO) – *Definition* A permanent function of an organization that embraces and practices Experience Management. – *Description* In large organizations, there may be several decentralized XMOs that are coordinated by a central XMO.

Finite Game – *Definition* A form of business with a clearly defined endpoint (like the end of a contract in a business context), and clear winners and losers. – *Description* The opposite of a finite game is an infinite game where parties work to keep the game going with a clear win-win commitment. [XV, XVI]

First Thing First – *Definition* An XLA practice that uses a two-by-two matrix to determine the highest priority based on customer or employee needs and the effort to deliver. – *Description* The goal is to decide what is evidently (a "no-brainer") the first priority to get things done.

First Time Right (FTR) – *Definition* A metric for whether something is done right the first time without rework to correct errors. – *Description* In the context of IT, FTR means the customer gets the correct answer, perfect delivery, or workable resolution after their first contact with a service or digital channel. The outcome is a satisfied customer without any waste of time and effort. It can be used as a KPI..

Fishbowl – *Definition* An XLA practices with an interview technique that gets unfiltered feedback from employees or customers. – *Description* An inner circle of interviewees discusses preselected topics while an outer circle of service providers observes silently and without taking notes. The inner circle then leaves, and the outer circle discusses the observed verbal and non-verbal (tone of voice and body language) communication.

Fit for Purpose – *Definition* A qualification of a digital product, application, or service that it is good enough to do the job. – *Description* Fit for purpose (F4P) is critical in determining if an economic investment enables employees to be productive. F4P is measured by the F4P XI. It focuses on the utility of a solution: its functionality. It is complemented by fit for use that focuses on the warranty.

Fit for Use – *Definition* A qualification of a digital product, application, or service that it will work well enough to do the job. – *Description* It focuses on the warranty of a solution: assurance regarding availability, performance, security etc. It is complemented by fit for purpose, which focuses on the utility.

Fixed Mindset – *Definition* An established set of attitudes with a tendency to avoid challenges, give up easily, provide negative feedback, and blame others. – *Description* It is the opposite of a growth mindset. [XVII]

Functional Value – *Definition* The second level within the elements of value pyramid that addresses economic and performance needs such as cost reduction and scalability.

Gap Analysis – *Definition* The result of an examination of the difference between the actual result and the desired result. – *Description* The difference can be either positive or negative.

Goal Setting Process – *Definition* The act of giving direction to the formulation of an ambition with concrete goals. – *Description* The goals are checked against the existing situation so that the goals are realistic and prioritized.

Golden Circle – *Definition* A model that proposes that organizations can only be truly successful if the so-called why is clear. – *Description* The model also includes what you do, and how you do what you do. [XVIII]

Gravity of Expectations – *Definition* A theory that states that the experience of a company's performance naturally declines over time. – *Description* Delivering the same good experience, without improvements or innovations, will not be good enough in the long run.

Growth Mindset – *Definition* An established set of attitudes with a tendency for praising and rewarding effort. – *Description* A growth mindset implies eagerness to tackle new challenges, face risks, and feel energized. People are praised and their efforts rewarded. It is the opposite of a fixed mindset. [xix]

ID10T – *Definition* An alternative spelling of the word idiot, used by technical people to refer to a human error when using technology: "I think this user has a code ID 10 T error." – *Description* Similar terms are UBD (user brain damage) or PICNIC (problem in chair, not in computer).

Individual Value – *Definition* The fourth level within the elements of value pyramid that addresses additional subjective elements, which can be both personal (attractive design) and work-related (network expansion).

Infinite Game – *Definition* A form of business where parties work to keep the game going with a clear win-win commitment. – *Description* The opposite is a finite game where there is a clearly defined endpoint (like the end of a contract in a business context), and there are clear winners and losers. [xx, xxi]

In-Scope Services – *Definition* The set of services or the part of the service for improvement of the experience.

Inspirational Value – *Definition* The fifth level within the elements of value pyramid that reinforces the vision and hope for the future such as easily moving to the next generation of technology and increases the social responsibility of a company.

In-Time Interaction – *Definition* A contact moment between a product or service and the customer.

In-Time Experience – *Definition* The experience that occurs during an in-time interaction.

Intrinsic Motivation – *Definition* The desire to take action that arises from factors within the individual rather than financial incentives, the avoidance of punishment, or other consequences.

Jobs to be Done – *Definition* A description of what someone wants to achieve by using a product or service. – *Description* It is a reframing of customer discovery based on why people choose to buy a product or service rather than on shared characteristics of a group of potential customers (aka personas). A JTBD can be formulated with the following structure: When I ... [situation], I want ... [motivation], so that ... [expected outcome]. [XXII]

Judgments – *Definition* Critical evaluations of events and people. [XXIII]

Key Performance Indicator (KPI) – *Definition* A desired target for objective performance measurement. – *Description* KPIs are based on O-data that have hypothesized correlations with SLA goals.

Key Proudness Indicator – *Definition* A KPI where performance has been replaced by proudness. – *Description* Key Proudness Indicators motivate people and are outcome-focused (what the business wants to achieve).

Key Value Indicator – *Definition* A Key Value Indicator is an actual number that for a team or organization, represents the impact from their actions

Killers of Potential Innovation – *Definition* KPI's that are used to protect the status quo, even when they have no value or even obstruct continuous improvement and innovation.

KPI Stress Testing – *Definition* The act of cross-checking the side effects of <u>Key Performance Indicators</u>. – *Description* The cure can sometimes be worse than the disease: metrics that produce a worse net result. Critical testing criteria are perverse incentives (undesirable behavior), negative impact (unwanted <u>outcomes</u>), and incompatibility (unintended negative coherence).

Landing Zone – *Definition* An XLA practice that helps to scheme and plot how users can land on the right spot. – *Description* The right spot can be defined as being happy or excited with a new application, device, portal, collaboration environment, chatbot, or any other service.

Landing Zone helps to think and act from an outside-in perspective. Landing Zone works exceptionally well for complex IT projects with higher levels of uncertainty in the case of user acceptance and user adoption.

Launch like Steve – *Definition* An XLA practice to plan the perfect introduction and celebration of new IT services and products. – *Description* The activity starts with Drama Day to visualize failure before flip-thinking to design Perfect Day.

Leary's Rose – *Definition* A model for human interactional behavior based on affect and power. – *Description* It is used for analyzing behavior when communication is difficult or when you want to improve collaboration. It helps to better understand someone and enables responding to that person's behavior more efficiently. [XXIV]

Line of Interaction – *Definition* A demarcation of activities that indicates when there is an interaction between customer and provider.

Line of Internal Interaction – *Definition* A demarcation of activities that indicates which activities are carried out by providers who are not directly responsible for interactions with the customer.

6. Glossary

Line of Visibility – *Definition* demarcation of activities that indicates which activities are visible to the customer and which are not.

Magic Zone – *Definition* A correlation of X-data (XLA) with O-data (SLA) that provides actionable insights for improving experience.

Major Projects – *Definition* A category of initiatives in the Action Priority Matrix that require a large investment but generate large improvements in experience.

MASTER Guideline – *Definition* A tool for prioritizing goals and making them tangible– *Description* MASTER stands fo r: Measurable, Achievable, Specific, Time-based, Energizing, and Relevant. "Energizing" extends the familiar SMART criteria.

Moment of Truth – *Definition* A critical interaction that makes or breaks the result from a business impact or Customer Experience perspective. – *Description* For mission-critical IT systems, these moments are commonly related to IT failure during daily, weekly, monthly, quarterly, or annual cycles. For customer journeys, these moments are often related to the peak-end rule.

Monetized Performance – *Definition* Achieved financial goals in terms of business growth and commercial position.

Moonshot Thinking – *Definition* A technique for finding a solution to a problem for which no logical solution can be thought of or for which a logical solution is too expensive. – *Description* A moonshot aims to achieve massive improvements in perception at a fraction of the cost of equivalent improvements.

Mr. Biv – *Definition* A proactive approach that can be used by teams as an early warning system to safeguard service excellence. – *Description* Mr. Biv is an acronym for Mistakes, Rework, Breakdowns, Inefficiencies, and Variations.
Source: Ritz-Carlton Hotel Company

N.E.R.D. (Necessary Executive Reshaping Degree) – *Definition* Reverse mentoring education to share knowledge and how-to's about technology and digital skills. – *Description* Many executives are fearful of revealing their lack of knowledge to junior employees. Addressed explicitly, open sharing can be incredibly rewarding and a game-changer for leadership.

Near Miss – *Definition* An incident that occurred but did not cause any serious damage, even though it had the potential to do so.

No Hassle – *Definition* A measure of how much effort it took an end user to get something done, solved, or answered after a service interaction. – *Description* Also referred to as Customer Effort Score (with reversed scores).

O-data – *Definition* Factual and objective performance measurements of IT systems, processes, and service interactions. – *Description* In the context of XLA, O-data is operational data collected from DEM and ITSM applications.

Onboarding – *Definition* The process of integrating a new hire into an organization and familiarizing the employee as an end-user with the (digital) services provided by the corporate functions. – *Description* Onboarding experience is measured by the Welcome XI.

OTOBOX – *Definition* An "On Xperience" extension of the traditional "On Time, On Budget" goal. – *Description* OTOBOX is an abbreviation of "On Time, On Budget, and On Xperience". Delivering a new application release or another user-impacting change "On Time, On Budget" doesn't mean the end-users will be happy and more productive with the change.

Outcome – *Definition* The result for a stakeholder, such as the value of a product or service for the customer. – *Description* Outcomes are often enabled by outputs. Sound output is always required but doesn't indicate if the business, employees', or customers' experience the value. Outcome always outclasses output.

Output – *Definition* The result of an activity, such as the quality and efficiency of the delivered product and service. – *Description* Outputs often enable outcomes. IT performance is traditionally measured with output metrics like reliability, latency, and availability. Output metrics too often mismatch with the actual impact of IT on the business and the Customer Experience.

Over-Time Experience – *Definition* A cumulative set of remembered in-time experiences of multiple interactions.

Peak-End Rule – *Definition* A theory explaining that people remember the most positive or negative moments ("peak") and the last moments ("end") of an experience better than other moments. – *Description* It is essential to improve the experience over time to make both the "peak" and the "end" positive. [xxv]

Persona – *Definition* A set of demographic and psychographic characteristics that represents a group of people who fulfill a role (e.g., customer, end user, service agent) within a certain organizational context, and is used for the purpose of serving that group effectively. – *Description* Also see jobs to be done as another customer discovery approach.

Perverse Incentive – *Definition* A goal or indicator that has an unintended and undesirable result, contrary to the intentions of the incentive designer.

Positioning – *Definition* A practice that provides insight into the current and desired perception of an organization – *Description* Positioning defines where a company's product (item or service) stands in relation to others offering similar products and services in the marketplace as well as in relation to the consumer. Good positioning makes a product unique and makes the consumer use it as it has a distinct benefit for them.

Positive Reinforcement – *Definition* Encouraging desired behavior by rewarding it.

Power Map – *Definition* A visualization of the interrelationships between individual stakeholders. – *Description* The Power Map helps to understand how stakeholders relate to each other, so you can quickly see how influence flows.

Priority Matrix – *Definition* A visualization of experience improvement initiatives based on four quadrants and two axes: improvement in experience and required investments.

Problem Zone – *Definition* A creative thinking space to observe and get insights into people's problems (diverging phase) to then determine the actual problem that needs solving (converging phase). – *Description* In IT, people often tend to jump to the solution zone and forget the importance of the problem zone.

Prototyping – *Definition* A development technique involving the presentation of a draft to stakeholders. – *Description* Prototyping can be used to predict how a service will be experienced without the delay and investment associated with the final version. It reduces risks and improves quality.

Purpose – *Definition* A reason for an organization's existence that aligns with long-term financial performance, provides a clear context for daily decision-making, and unifies and motivates relevant stakeholders.

6. Glossary

Quality of Experience (QoE) – *Definition* A measure of the delight or annoyance of a customer with a service. Netflix embraced QoE, focusing on Customer Experience, quantified by metrics like video load time, visual quality, and rate of video interruptions. – *Description* Also see Quality of Service.

Quality of Services (QoS) – *Definition* The description or measurement in networking for the overall technical performance of a service layer. – *Description* QoS is used to ensure traffic quality management, like internet-protocol networking. The problem with QoS is that it is not about the Quality of Experience (QoE) from a customer perspective.

Quick Wins – *Definition* A category of initiatives in the Action Priority Matrix that require low investment but generate large improvements in experience.

RACI – *Definition* A matrix for clarifying roles and responsibilities in collaboration and decision-making. – *Description* The acronym stands for Responsible, Accountable, Consulted and Informed. RACIs are essential to collaborating effectively when the stakeholders are interdependent to achieve the desired outcome.

Rational Compassion – *Definition* A logical analysis of the costs and benefits of empathy, without the irrational, impulsive, and sometimes cruel downside of empathy. – *Description* Empathy can have a negative effect on moral judgments. By removing emotional involvement, better and more rational decisions can be taken about how to meet the needs of people.

Also see empathy and sympathy. [XXVI]

Real User Monitoring (RUM) – *Definition* The type of technology that measures User Experience from the perspective of the application. – *Description* This includes the health of an internal B2B application or B2C website up until the detailed level of monitoring the performance of the functionality (buttons, search fields, forms) of the applications. [XXVII]

Return on Experience (ROX) – *Definition* ROX is a metric used to measure the value derived from investments in experience management. – *Description* To calculate ROX, the monetized benefits are divided by the cost of the investment in XM. Within XLA, the ROX evaluates the business case. ROX is the equivalent of Return on Investment (ROI), a popular profitability metric used to evaluate how well an investment has performed.

Reverse Brainstorming – *Definition* An XLA practice that builds on our natural ability to see problems faster than solutions. – *Description* Instead of asking a group to brainstorm on ideas that would work, the group has to come up with ways that could cause a plan, project, or product introduction to fail.

Righting Reflex – *Definition* An almost automatic reaction to try to help another by giving a solution to a problem, even if the other person is not looking for it yet. – *Description* The other person only wants to be heard. The more you try to fix someone's problem and push that solution, the more unfavorable the response.

Service – *Definition* Economic exchange where actors in the role of service providers and service consumers collaborate to co-create value for mutual benefit.

Scope – *Definition* The first step in the Define phase of the Experience Management Journey. – *Description* efine gives direction and helps to create focus on the in-scope services, the business you are in, the partners you work with and the roles you hold within your team.

Secrets, Lies, and Assumptions – *Definition* An alternative explanation of the abbreviation SLA (Service Level Agreement). – *Description* Traditional SLAs have nothing to do with the quality experienced by the user or performance in real business life.

Service Blueprint – *Definition* A visualization of the connection between Customer Experience and an organization's way of working. It connects internal processes with customer actions and visualizes the mutual relationship.

Service Chain – *Definition* A set of organizations in the ecosystem that are connected by provider-consumer relationships.

Service Design – *Definition* The activity that helps to design, innovate or improve services to make them more useful and usable for customers, and more efficient and effective for organizations.

Service Improvement Plan (SIP) – *Definition* A formal plan to implement improvements to services.

Service Level Agreement (SLA) – *Definition* A documented agreement between a service provider and a customer that identifies both the services required and the expected level of those services.

Solution Zone – *Definition* A creative thinking space that specifies all the potential solutions (diverging phase) and focuses on the probable solutions (converging phase).

Sore Loser Agreement – *Definition* An alternative explanation of the abbreviation SLA (Service Level Agreement). – *Description* The word "loser" applies to a service provider who meets the minimum service requirements – stated in the SLAs – but is not valued and rewarded by their customers.

Stakeholder Map – *Definition* A visualization of internal and external stakeholders based on their interest to improve experience compared to their influence.

Stickiness – *Definition* A description of the attractiveness of an application or software feature for the customer. – *Description* High stickiness implies more value and deeper engagement.

Survey Fatigue – *Definition* Respondents' lack of motivation to participate in or complete surveys.

Switchtracking – *Definition* The act of deliberately changing the subject during a conversation. – *Description* People often start arguing separate points back and forth with no mutual understanding or resolution. [xxviii] Switchtracking often happens in conversations where feedback is given.

Sympathy – *Definition* The ability to feel the feelings of others. It is based on the recipient's own emotions. They care about and are sorry for someone else's feelings. – *Description* The recipient does not just understand the other person's feelings – they share them. Also see empathy and rational compassion.

Synthetic Transaction Monitoring (STM) – *Definition* The type of technology that helps organizations proactively test services such as saas, websites, Daas, Iaas, Paas. [xxix]

System Requirements – *Definition* Descriptions of the needs that the system should fulfill so developers can build the system. – *Description* They are either functional (UTILITY) or non-functional (WARRANTY). The rule of thumb is that functionals start with "the system does…" and non-functionals with "the system is…"

Table Stakes – *Definition* The first level within the Elements of value pyramid that meet minimum specifications at an acceptable price, are compliant with regulations, and meet ethical standards.

Task Force – *Definition* A temporary team that adopts, practices and improves Experience Management. – *Description* The goal of a Task Force is to rapidly improve experience and collaboration that generates business impact, both inside and outside the organization. It remains in effect until Experience Management becomes business-as-usual with a roadmap, processes, and governance (evaluate, direct, monitor) in place. At that point, responsibility is transferred to an XMO. For continuity, Task Force members may staff the XMO, at least for its initial period of operation.

Thankless Tasks – *Definition* A category of initiatives in the Action Priority Matrix that require a large investment but generate little improvement in experience.

Theory of Mind – *Definition* An essential understanding that other people can have different mental states. – *Description* It involves thinking about mental states, and the cognitive ability to sense <u>emotions</u>, desires, beliefs, and knowledge.

User Adoption – *Definition* The process of ensuring that end users (employees or customers) are successful in using digital products, applications, or services. – *Description* In Enterprise IT, user adoption is often related to the transition from one system to another. As a metric, user adoption is part of the XI Library.

User Brain Damage – *Definition* A term that service agents or developers use to refer to a question or human error. – *Description* There are many reasons for mistakes that experts quickly oversee due to their expert bias. Having a beginner's mindset helps solve problems.

User Experience (UX) – *Definition* The end user's thoughts, feelings, and impressions. – *Description* The term UX is primarily used in IT and is related to the end-user (employee) or the interactions of people (customers) with a digital product or service. Also see Customer Experience.

User Requirements – *Definition* The narrative of what users want and need from the system to establish whether the right customer problem is being solved. – *Description* Even when users provide incomplete, inaccurate, and self-conflicting information, user requirements are the key to success.

Watermelon Effect – *Definition* A situation where service providers show "green" (positive) performance indicators, but the customer's emotions are colored "red" (negative). – *Description* The watermelon effect kicks in because traditional performance indicators such as availability, network latency, and resolution times are abracadabra for business stakeholders and end-users.

Welcome – *Definition* A signature Experience Indicator to measure employee and customer feedback on the onboarding experience.

WhoDo Game – *Definition* An XLA practice that produces a list of who is going to do what with regards to all the tasks needed to realize greater business impact by driving and improving collaboration and experience.

Win-Win – *Definition* A situation where the outcome benefits all parties involved. – *Description* Each party is happy with the outcome because everyone wins; there are no losers.

X-data – *Definition* Subjective measurements of human perception of IT systems, processes, service interactions, and business impact. – *Description* X-data covers a wide variety of themes such as user adoption, usability, and satisfaction.

6. Glossary

XI Library – *Definition* A collection of Xperience indicators that can be used to measure human experience within a defined context. – *Description* The library covers a wide variety of experience themes, such as the modern workspace, user adoption, onboarding, and omni- channel support.

XLA 6P Framework – *Definition* Structured guidance that helps organizations improve the impact of IT services on people and their business. – *Description* The framework comprises a way of thinking (perspectives), a way of working (practices and products), and a way of being (people, principles and propositions).

XLA – *Definition* An outcome-oriented document; a measurable and verifiable agreement between the IT provider and the customer with respect to collaboration, experience, and business impact (the three XLA value drivers).

XLA Elements – *Definition* The set of XLA Strategy, XLA Roadmap, and XLA Governance. – *Description* Also see XLA Framework (NEN).

XLA Framework (NEN) – *Definition* A set of interrelated value drivers, elements and success factors to base an XLA organization on in which the XLAs can be implemented and executed.
Source: NTA 8038:2020

XLA Goal – *Definition* The desired conditions of each of the XLA value drivers. – *Description* XLA Goals are derived from the organization's ambitions.

XLA Governance – *Definition* A framework of decision-making and responsibilities to continuously focus management efforts on the XLA Strategy and XLA Roadmap.

XLA Mindset – *Definition* The conviction that it is possible to let go of old belief systems and traditional managerial reflexes to adopt the new way of working with XLA.

XLA People – *Definition* The organizational function that works with XLA. – *Description* This is an element of the XLA 6P Framework.

XLA Perspectives – *Definition* Ways of thinking for value-creation with XLA. – *Description* his is an element of the XLA 6P Framework.

XLA Practice Areas – *Definition* Areas of work for managing the impact of IT services on people and their business, within which XLA Practices are applied.

XLA Practices – *Definition* Guidance on how to adopt and execute XLA. – *Description* This is an element of the XLA 6P Framework.

XLA Principles – *Definition* Assumptions that enable and constrain behavior in the XLA domain. – *Description* This is an element of the XLA 6P Framework.

XLA Products – *Definition* Digital resources that support the way of working with XLA. – *Description* This is an element of the XLA 6P Framework.

XLA Propositions – *Definition* Reasons for adopting XLA. – *Description* This is an element of the XLA 6P Framework.

XLA Roadmap – *Definition* A document with initiatives in a logical sequence that put the XLA strategy into practice and measure the progress of the achievement of the strategy. – *Description* The XLA Roadmap describes the necessary initiatives that enable the ambition from the XLA strategy to be achieved.

XLA Skillset – *Definition* A set of skills that is needed to implement and execute new thinking from the XLA Mindset.

XLA Stack – *Definition* A visual representation of how the correlation of X-data and O-data provides insight into how to measure the achievement of the desired experience.

XLA Strategy – *Definition* A document that communicates how an organization intends to use experience to successfully differentiate itself from its competition. – *Description* The differentiation can be found in the choice of customers the organization serves, their organization's products and services, or their processes.

XLA Success Factors – *Definition* The combination of mindset, skillset, and toolset needed for taking action in the organization. – *Description* Also see XLA Framework (NEN).

XLA Toolset – *Definition* A set of tools that is needed in order to get a sufficient understanding of, and to focus management efforts on, collaboration, experience and business impact. It often includes software applications.

XLA Value Drivers – *Definition* Experience, collaboration, and business impact – *Description* Also see XLA Framework (NEN).

Xperience – *Definition* An alternative spelling of the word experience.

Xperience Level Agreement (XLA) – *Definition* An outcome-oriented document that is a measurable and verifiable agreement between the IT provider and the customer with respect to collaboration, experience, and business impact. – *Description* An XLA can be an integral part of an SLA, an addition to an SLA, or a separate document that overrides an SLA.

Zero Repeat – *Definition* A concept focused on learning from mistakes and taking out the root cause of a problem to prevent the problem from occurring again. – *Description* Strong leadership is required to use this concept as a KPI to enable a safe learning culture.

Zone of Good Enough – *Definition* The range of acceptable quality levels to prevent terrible experience, and renounce delightful customer experiences.

I. Broeder, R. den, & Kerkhofs, J. (2020), Organizational Behavior Management, an introduction.
II. Skinner, B.F. (1938), The Bhavior of Organisms.
III. IIBA's BABOK.
IV. Design Council (2005).
V. Bangera, M., Byrne, P., and Siegfried, G. (2022), Gartner Market Guide for Digital Experience Monitoring.
VI. Design Council (2005).
VII. Design Council (2005).
VIII. Rogers, E.M. (2006), Diffusion of Innovations.
IX. Almquist, E., Senior, J., and Bloch, N. (2016), The Elements of Value. Measuring—and Delivering—What Consumers Really Want in HBR Magazine (September 2016).
X. American Psychological Association dictionary.
XI. Bangera, M., Byrne, P., and Siegfried, G. (2022), Gartner Market Guide for Digital Experience Monitoring.
XII. American Psychological Association dictionary.
XIII. Pine II, B.J. and Gilmore, J.H (1998), Welcome to the Experience Economy, in HBR Magazine (July–August 1998).
XIV. American Psychological Association dictionary.
XV. Sinek, S. (2019), The Infinite Game.
XVI. Carse, James P. (1987), Finite and Infinite Games.
XVII. Dweck, C.S., (2006), Mindset: The New Psychology of Success.
XVIII. Sinek, S. (2006), TED Talk How Great Leaders Inspire Action.
XIX. Dweck, C.S., (2006), Mindset: The New Psychology of Success.
XX. Sinek, S. (2019), The Infinite Game.
XXI. Carse, James P. (1987), Finite and Infinite Games.
XXII. Christensen, C.M. et al (2016), Know Your Customers' "Jobs to Be Done" in HBR Magazine (September 2016).

XXIII. American Psychological Association dictionary.

XXIV. Leary, T. (1957), Interpersonal Diagnosis of Personality: A Functional Theory and Methodology for Personality Evaluation.

XXV. The Peak-End Rule is an elaboration on the snapshot model of remembered utility proposed by Daniel Kahneman and Barbara Frederickson.

XXVI. Bloom, P. (2016), Against Empathy: The Case for Rational Compassion.

XXVII. Bangera, M., Byrne, P., and Siegfried, G. (2022), Gartner Market Guide for Digital Experience Monitoring.

XXVIII. Heen, S. and Stone, D. (2014), Thanks for the Feedback: The Science and Art of Receiving Feedback Well.

XXIX. Bangera, M., Byrne, P., and Siegfried, G. (2022), Gartner Market Guide for Digital Experience Monitoring.

XXX. Inspired by Syco Entertainment's television music competition The X Factor, that refers to the undefinable "something" that makes for star quality.

Acknowledgements

It's not the lone nut but the followers who spark a movement. Together we ignited something special. In 2015, "XLA as a philosophy" was presented by Marco Gianotten at the world's premier IT Service Management in Las Vegas: PINK. What happens in Vegas never really stays in Vegas.

Fast forward to now. With good and emergent practices, we are on to something. We thank the fantastic editorial team for this XLA Pocketbook: Marthijn Brouwer, Karel Helsen, Rob Herings, Justin Mensah, Marsha Muller, Anke van de Kerkhof, Karen Noorda, Laurie Treffers, and Bart Verbrugge were indispensable in shaping thoughts and models.

Einstein's witty quote on problem-solving is: "Insanity is doing the same thing over and over and expecting different results." Wicked problems in tech often require a radically different approach. Many tech leaders and professionals believed in the concept of XLA. We started to build the plane while flying, empowered by tens of companies who gave us the benefit of the doubt.

The co-creation and development of good practices and the XLA methodology will help others in the future. We owe many thanks to those who supported us, gave us the benefit of the doubt, or hired us to flip-think and fix problems in unconventional ways: Peter Aalbers, Bill Barrett, Manon Van Beek, Arie Van Bennekom, Pim Berger, Saul Van Beurden, Bas Bremmer, Gerhard Van der Bijl, Jette Van Eldijk, Raphaël

Hélion, Dave Van Herpen, Julian Hessels, Mel Jacobs, Herald Jongen, Arnold Kamphuis, Neil Keating, Frank Keessen, Anneke Keller, Hans Koolen, André Van der Linden, Alan Nance, Michel Peters, Bart Van Reeken, Emile Stam, Francisca Alcaide Soler, Jeroen Tas, Michiel Valk, Janine Vos, and Patrick Wit.

Amsterdam, February 2023
Marco Gianotten & Mark Smalley

"The first follower is actually an underestimated form of leadership in itself. The first follower is what transforms a lone nut into a leader."
— Derek Sivers